George Burlingame Denison

A record of the descendants of Samuel Denison

With notices of his ancestry, commencing with William Denison, who

came to America in 1631

George Burlingame Denison

A record of the descendants of Samuel Denison
With notices of his ancestry, commencing with William Denison, who came to America in 1631

ISBN/EAN: 9783337113742

Printed in Europe, USA, Canada, Australia, Japan

Cover: Foto ©ninafisch / pixelio.de

More available books at **www.hansebooks.com**

OF THE DESCENDANTS OF

SAMUEL DENISON,

LATE OF FLOYD, ONEIDA CO., N. Y., WITH NOTICES OF HIS
ANCESTRY, COMMENCING WITH

WILLIAM DENISON,

WHO CAME TO AMERICA IN 1631, AND SETTLED IN ROXBURY, MASS

PREPARED BY

GEORGE BURLINGAME DENISON,

MUSCATINE, IOWA.

PREFACE.

THE preparation of a record of my father's family has been inspired by the perusal of a record of the descendants of Captain George Denison, of Stonington, Conn. (of whom my father was one), prepared and published by John Denison Baldwin, of Worcester, Mass., and Rev. William Clift, of Mystic Bridge, Conn., grandsons, respectively, of Sarah Denison Baldwin and Anna Denison Clift, who were daughters of John and Abigal Avery Denison, of Stonington, Conn. This John was the great grandson of Captain George Denison.

Originally, my intention was to commence with and give the record of the family of my grandfather Daniel Denison, Jr., and Catharine Avery, his wife, who migrated from New London, Conn., and settled at Stephentown, N. Y., in 1771; but I have found it impossible to get the information necessary to compile a full and correct record. I believe the record of my father's family is absolutely correct and complete.

Such information as I have been able to obtain of the families of my father's brothers and sisters I have inserted.

By the permission of Messrs. Baldwin and Clift, I have borrowed largely from their admirable Genealogy of the Denison family; indeed, except for them the result of my labor would appear insignificant. They are particularly entitled to the thanks of the descendants of Captain George Denison and I have assured them they have mine.

GEORGE BURLINGAME DENISON.

MUSCATINE, IOWA, *February*, 1884.

THE FIRST GENERATION.

WILLIAM DENISON, born in England about 1586, came to America in 1631, and settled in Roxbury, Mass., having with him his wife Margaret, his three sons, Daniel, Edward and George, and John Elliott, who seems to have been a tutor in his family. Mr. Elliott became pastor of the church in Roxbury, and did missionary work among the Indians. Mr. Denison was a deacon of the Roxbury church. He had been liberally educated, and his sons were carefully educated. He died in Roxbury, Jan. 25, 1653; his wife died there, Feb. 23, 1645.

> Daniel, born in 1612, died 1682.
> Edward, born in 1614, married Elizabeth Welde.
> **GEORGE**, born in 1618, married Bridget Thompson and Ann Borodell.

THE SECOND GENERATION.

1. Daniel Denison (son of William), born in 1612, was married to Patience Dudley, daughter of Gov. Thomas Dudley, and lived at Ipswich, Mass., and had two children : John, who married a daughter of Deputy Governor John Symonds ; and Elizabeth, who married John Rogers, president of Harvard College. He was very prominent in Massachusetts, having been Major General of Militia, Speaker of the House of Representatives, and for 29 years one of the "Assistants." He died in 1682. It is supposed, but not absolutely certain, that his last male descendant bearing the family name, was an accomplished young clergyman, who died at Ipswich, unmarried, Aug. 25, 1747.

2. Edward Denison (son of William), born in 1614, was married to Elizabeth Welde, of Roxbury, and had twelve children. He lived in Roxbury, where he was a man of mark, and died there, April 26, 1668 ; his wife died there in 1716, aged 91 years. His children are :

> Elizabeth, born in 1642.
> John, born in 1644.
> Edward, born and died in 1645.
> Joseph, born and died in 1646.
> Jeremiah, born in 1647, and died 1649.
> Margaret, born in 1650, married D. Mason.
> Mary, born in 1653.
> Hannah, born in 1655.
> Sarah, born in 1657.
> Deborah, born in 1660, died in 1667.
> William, born in 1664.
> Deborah, born in 1666, died 1667.

Edward Denison's son William, married Dorothy

Welde, of Roxbury, and had children; but it is not known to those who have inquired carefully that any male descendants of this family, bearing the family name are now living.

3. George Denison (son of William), born in 1618, was married, first, in 1640, to Bridget Thompson, daughter of "John Thompson, *gent.*, of Preston, Northamptonshire, England," whose widow Alice had come to America, and was living in Roxbury. She had in this country, besides Bridget, these three sons: John Thompson; Anthony Thompson, recorded in New Haven, Conn., in 1643, as a planter; and William Thompson, who died in New Haven in 1683. George and Bridget (Thompson) Denison had two children born in Roxbury; Sarah, born March 20, 1641, married Thomas Stanton, Jr.; Hannah, born May 20, 1643, twice married.

The wife, Bridget, died in 1643. George Denison then went to England, served under Cromwell in the army of the Parliament, won distinction, was wounded at Naseby, was nursed at the house of John Borodell, by his daughter Ann, was married to Ann, returned to Roxbury, and finally settled at Stonington, Conn. The children of George and Ann (Borodell) Denison were as follows:

> **JOHN**, born July 14, 1646; married Phebe Lay.
> Ann, born May 20, 1649; married Gershom Palmer.
> Borodell, born in 1651; married Samuel Stanton.
> George, born in 1653; married Mercy Gorham.
> William, born in 1655; married Sarah Stanton.
> Margaret, born in 1657; married James Brown, jr.
> Mercy, born in 1659; died March 10, 1671.

George Denison died in Hartford, Oct. 23, 1694,

while there on some special business, being 76 years
old.   His wife, Ann Borodell, died Sept. 26, 1712, aged
97 years.   They were both remarkable for magnificent
personal appearance, and for force of mind and character.   She was always called "Lady Ann."   They held
a foremost place in Stonington.   At the time of their
marriage, in 1645, she was 30 years old and he 27.   He
has been described as "the Miles Standish of the settlement," but he was a greater and more brilliant soldier
than Miles Standish.   He had no equal in any of the
colonies, for conducting a war against the Indians, ex-
cepting, perhaps, Captain John Mason.   Miss Calkins, in her history of New London, says of him :
"Our early history presents no character of bolder and
more active spirit than Captain George Denison; he
reminds us of the border men of Scotland."   In emer-
gencies he was always in demand, and he was almost
constantly placed in important public positions.

THE THIRD GENERATION.

John Denison (son of George and grandson of William Denison), born July 14, 1646, was married Nov. 26, 1667, to Phebe Lay, daughter of Robert and Sarah Lay, of Saybrook, Conn. The marriage contract or deed of settlement, arranged between their parents, is recorded in Saybrook. By this deed of settlement, executed before the marriage, the respective parents conveyed to John Denison and Phebe Lay the farm granted to Captain George Denison near the mouth of Mystic river in Stonington, and the house and land in Saybrook, which Mr. Lay had formerly bought of John Post. This deed was witnessed by Rev. Simon Bradstreet, and "Ann Denison, Jr." They settled in Stonington, on "the farm near the mouth of Mystic River." He was known as "Captain John Denison," held a prominent position in Stonington, and in many ways was a man of mark. He died in 1698, aged 52 years. His wife died in 1699, aged 49. Their children were:

John, born Jan. 1, 1669 ; lived in Saybrook.
GEORGE, born March 28, 1671 ; lived in New London.
Robert, born Sept. 17, 1673 ; lived in Mohegan.
William, born April 7, 1677 ; lived in North Stonington.
Daniel, born March 28, 1680 ; lived in Stonington.
Samuel, born Feb. 23, 1683 ; died May 12, 1683.
Ann, born Oct. 3, 1684 ; twice married.
Phebe, born April 6, 1690 ; married Ebenezar Billings, Jr.
Sarah, born July 20, 1692 ; married Isaac Williams.

1*

THE FOURTH GENERATION.

George Denison (son of Captain John Denison, and great grandson of William), was born March 28, 1671. He graduated from Harvard College, studied law and settled in New London, Conn., where he was town clerk, county clerk, and clerk of probate. He was married in 1694, to Mrs. Mary (Wetherell) Harris (daughter of Daniel Wetherell, a very prominent citizen of New London, who was born in Maidstone, County Kent, England, Nov. 29, 1630, and died in New London, April 14, 1719). George Denison died Jan. 22, 1720. His wife died Aug. 22, 1711. Their children were:

Grace, born March 4, 1695 ; married Edward Hallam.
Phebe, born March 6, 1697 ; married Gibson Harris.
Hannah, born March 28, 1699 ; married John Hough.
Borodell, born May 17, 1701 ; married Jonathan Latimer.
DANIEL, born June 27, 1703 ; married Rachel Starr.
Wetherell, born Aug. 24, 1705 ; married Lydia Moore.
Ann, born Aug. 15, 1707 ; twice married.
Sarah, born June 20, 1710 ; married Wm. Douglas.

THE FIFTH GENERATION.

Daniel Denison (son of George Denison, great great grandson of William Denison), born June 27, 1703, was married to Rachel Starr, Nov. 14, 1726, and lived in New London, Conn. He died previous to 1760, and his widow, about 1760, married Col. Ebenezar Avery, of South Groton, who had twelve children by his first wife, Lucy Latham. Rachel (Starr) Denison, had ten children by her first husband. Daniel Denison, Jr., married Col. Ebenezer's daughter Katherine, previous to his mother's second marriage, and Phebe married his son Ebenezar Avery, Jr. Mrs. Rachel died in 1791, aged 86 years. The children of Daniel and Rachel (Starr) Denison were as follows:

Mary, born Aug. 19, 1728; twice married.
DANIEL, born Dec., 16, 1730; married Katherine Avery.
Thomas, born Nov. 4, 1732; married Katherine Starr.
Rachel, born Sept. 20, 1734; married Joseph Copp.
Samuel, born Nov. 9, 1736; died in 1767; no family.
Hannah, born Jan. 2, 1739; married Henry Jepson.
Ann, born Sept. 18, 1743; died 1767.
Phebe, born Sept. 18, 1743; married Ebenezer Avery, Jr.
James, born April 18, 1746; married Esther Brown.
Elizabeth, born Nov. 19, 1748; married John Barker.

THE SIXTH GENERATION.

Record of the family of Daniel Denison, Jr., including his children and grandchildren only.

Daniel Denison, Jr. (son of Daniel Denison, and great great great grandson of William Denison), born in New London, Conn., Dec. 16, 1730 ; was married to Katherine Avery, July 1, 1756, who was a daughter of Col. Ebenezer Avery by his first wife. They settled in New London, where they lived until 1771, when they moved into the wilderness of New York, and settled in the town of Stephentown, Rensselaer County, east of Albany. He was one of the prominent men of the new settlement ; held some important positions conferred upon him by the partiality of the citizens of the new settlement. By an act of the Legislature he was appointed one of three commissioners to adjust disputes of boundaries between the settlers. We make this extract from a memorandum book which he kept, and now in the hands of his grandson, Jonathan Denison, of South Berlin, N. Y.: "June 1771, I moved into this county from New London, and brought with me nine children." He died in 1793, and his wife died in 1825, aged 88 years. They were both buried in the family burying-ground in Berlin. The homestead remained in the family upward of 90 years. They had thirteen children, as follows :

1. Katherine, born July 24, 1757 ; married James Jones.
2. Daniel, born Sept. 26, 1758 ; married Hannah Jones.
3. Ebenezer, born Jan. 26, 1760 ; married Widow Jones.
4. Jonathan, born May 17, 1761 ; married Sarah Green.
5. George, born April 12, 1763 ; died in 1786.

6. Griswold, born Aug. 21, 1765 ; married Rhoda Tifft.
7. Aseneth, born Feb. 24, 1767 ; married Roger Jones.
8. David, born March 19, 1769 ; married Widow Williams.
9. Latham, born March 8, 1771 ; married Elenor Tifft.
10. A child, unnamed, born and died Aug. 18, 1773.
11. **SAMUEL**, born Oct. 24, 1774 ; twice married.
12. Elihu, born April 14, 1777; married Thankful Stewart.
13. Thomas, born May 5, 1779 ; married Polly Cary.

1. Katherine Denison (daughter of Daniel Denison, Jr.), born July 24, 1757, was married to James Jones, and lived in Stephentown. He died in 1803, and she died in 1850. Their children were:

> James H., born March 28, 1799 ; married and lived in Illinois. Their other children are: Katherine ; Eunice ; Jerusha ; Daniel ; William ; Rachel ; Avery ; Elias ; and Clarissa. This is all we know of Katherine's children.

2. Daniel Denison (son of Daniel Denison, Jr.) was born Sept. 26, 1758, and married Hannah Jones in 1780. They settled in Stephentown, and afterward moved to Seneca County, N. Y. He died July 22, 1832, and she died Feb. 14, 1832. Their children are :

> Daniel, born Feb. 18, 1785, and died young.
> George, born Aug. 25, 1786 ; died Sept. 12, 1825.
> Hannah, born March 11, 1788 ; died young.
> Rev. Avery, born June 28, 1790 ; married Mercy L. Benedict, and had eleven children. He was a Baptist clergyman, settled in Michigan, where his descendants mostly reside.
> Eunice, born Dec. 10, 1791 ; married Edward Briggs.
> Clarissa, born Aug. 23, 1793 ; died in 1812.
> Elias, born Oct. 19, 1795 ; died in 1848.
> Nancy, born March 20, 1797 ; married David Lightbody. Lived at Seneca Falls, N. Y., and had nine children.
> Daniel, born May 12, 1799 ; died April 13, 1812.

Lorena, born Feb., 1802.

Hannah, born Dec. 1, 1803 ; died March 7, 1822.

Rhoda, born May 22, 1805 ; married Jerry Bement ; they
lived in Rochester, N. Y., and had seven children.

Delina, born Oct. 27, 1809 ; died Oct. 13, 1827.

3. Ebenezer, A. (son of Daniel Denison, Jr.), born
Jan. 26, 1760, was married in 1784 to Mrs. Elizabeth
(Spencer) Jones. They lived in Berne, Albany County,
N. Y. Their children are :

Katherine, born in 1786.

Ebenezer, A., Jr., born 1788 ; married Esther Gallup ;
lived at Rutherford Park, N. J.; had six children.

Hannah, born in 1790 ; married Isaac Allen.

Polly, born in 1792 ; married William Allen.

William, born in 1795.

Alma, born in 1797.

Orpha, born in 1799 ; married Eugene Wood.

Avery, born in 1802.

4. Jonathan Denison (son of Daniel Denison, Jr.),
born May 17, 1761, was married to Sarah Green in 1786.
They lived in Berlin on the homestead. Their children
are :

James, born Oct. 19, 1789 ; married Esther Green ; had
five children.

Daniel, born Dec. 11, 1791 ; married Isabell Niles ; lived
at Berlin and had seven children.

Benjamin G., born Oct. 30, 1793 ; married Abigal Babcock ;
lived in Greenbush, N. Y., and had four children.

Polly, born Nov. 14, 1798 ; married Holden Sweet ; had
three children.

A son born and died Dec. 9, 1801.

Gorham, born April 19, 1806 ; twice married ; lived in Berlin and had eight children.

Eri, born Nov. 10, 1807 ; died Oct. 21, 1808.

> David, twin, born Dec. 22, 1809 ; married Abigal Maxon;
> lived in Delaware County, N. Y.; had three children.
> Jonathan, twin, born Dec. 22, 1809 ; married Elzina Allen;
> lived in Berlin, N. Y., and had four children.

6. Griswold Denison (son of Daniel Denison, Jr.), born Aug. 21, 1765, was married in 1793, to Rhoda Tifft. They lived in Stephentown, N. Y. She died March 22, 1869, aged 91 years. Their children are:

> George T., born March 17, 1795.
> Rebecca, born in 1797; married Emerson Hull.
> Alson, born in 1798; died young.

7. Asenath Denison (daughter of Daniel Denison, Jr.), born Feb. 24, 1767, married Roger Jones ; lived in Berlin, Albany County, N. Y. They had twelve children as follows :

> Eliphalet, Asenath, Denison, Latham, Sally, Drusilla, Katherine, Avery, Alanson, William, Alva and Nancy.

This is all we know of Asenath's family.

8. David Denison (son of Daniel Denison, Jr.), born March 19, 1769, married in 1794, to Mrs. Polly (Jones) Williams. They lived in Kortright, Delaware County, N. Y., and had these children:

> Polly, born in 1795.
> Orrel, born in 1797.
> Ansel, born in 1799.
> Caroline, born in 1800.
> Furman, born in 1802.

9. Latham Denison (son of Daniel Denison, Jr.), born in New London, Conn., March 8, 1771 ; married Elenor Tifft, Nov. 20, 1796. She was born Jan. 13, 1780. In 1800, he moved into the wilderness in the town of Floyd, Oneida County, N. Y., where he continued to reside

until his death in 1847. She died in 1846. Their
children are :

> Holly, born Nov. 21, 1797; died young.
>
> Pedy, born in 1799 ; died young.
>
> Terressa, born April 10, 1800; married David Martin ;
> both dead.
>
> George, born March 31, 1802; died young.
>
> Rhoda, born Jan. 28, 1804; married Alfred Martin, April
> 20, 1820; he is dead and she lives in Rome, N. Y.
>
> Alonzo, born March 15, 1806; married first, Mary Knox,
> she is dead; married second time, Sarah Hughsted.
> They live in Rome, N. Y.
>
> Halsey, born Feb. 24, 1808 ; died young.
>
> Pedy, born Jan. 3, 1810; married Lansing W. Cole.
>
> George T., born Jan. 23, 1812; married Arabella Davis;
> lives in Delta, Oneida County, N. Y.
>
> Angeline, born May 9, 1816; married first, Henderson
> Trip; was divorced, then married Jackson Clark ;
> lives in Delta, N. Y.
>
> Wellington, born Jan. 29, 1822; married Rhoda A. Cole ;
> he died Jan. 17, 1881, and she lives in Rome, N. Y.

LATHAM DENISON'S GRANDCHILDREN.

Terressa (Denison) Martin's children :

> Melissa, married Alva Colman; live in Mich.
>
> Harvey, married Rhoda Denison.
>
> George, married Mary Carpenter ; both dead.
>
> Elenor, married James Cochron; live in Wis.
>
> Avery, married Emeline Lewis; live in Ohio.
>
> Jane, married James Conklin; live in Ill.
>
> Rhoda, married James Denison; live in Penn.
>
> Helen, married Wm. Edgerton; live in Wis.
>
> Rose Ann and Delevan, twins ; both dead.
>
> Theodore, married Catharine Lusher; live on homestead,
> Western N. Y.
>
> Denison, twice married ; lives in Wis.

Rhoda (Denison) Martin's children :

Chester, died in Milwaukee, Wis.
Laura, married Jonathan Stewart; live in Minn.
Latham, married Diantha Bliss; live in Wis.
Elvira, married Geo. W. Cole; live at Byron, N. Y.
Rhoda, married D. C. Jefferson; live in Wis.
Adeline, married J. E. Wilcox; live at Ridge Mills, N. Y.
Angeline, married Wm. Hicks; live at Delta, N. Y.
Emily, married H. H. Moulton; live in Charleston, S. C.
Jane, married Joel Williams; live at Ridge Mills, N. Y.
Lyman, married Jane Bowman; live in Rome, N. Y.
Clark, married Harriet Hicks; live in Ill.
Amanda, married J. P. Mattoon; live at Vienna, N. Y.
Charles, married Maria France; live in Neb.

Alonzo Denison's children :

Elenor, married Charles Benedict ; is dead.
Elizabeth, married Wm. C. Fox; lives in South Troy, Wis.
Latham, married Ellen Wightman; lives in South Troy,
    Wis.
Mary Ann, married Orrin Pencil ; lives in South Troy, Wis.
Angeline, married A. J. Anderson ; is dead.
Rhoda ; died young.
Ida, by second wife ; died young.

Pedy (Denison) Cole's children :

Lysander, married Elvira Wilkeson ; live in Rome, N. Y,
Adaline, married —— Hoskins ; live in Minn.
Jane, married Latham Denison ; live in South Troy, Minn.
Angeline, married Homer Tiffany ; live in Turen, N. Y.
Matteson, married —— Roberts ; live in Port Leyden, N. Y.
Lansing ; lives in Iowa.
Samuel, married Rosa Lewis ; lives in Auburn, N. Y.
Ellen, married —— Allen ; lives in Wis.
Pedy, married —— Smith ; lives in Houseville, N. Y.
Medora, married —— Smyder ; lives in Saratoga, N. Y.
Latham ; died young.
Halsey ; lives in Washington T'y.

George T. Denison's children :

> George W.; married Elizabeth Fraser ; lives in Delta, N.Y.
>
> Latham M., married Hellen Berry ; lives at Peterboro',
> N. Y.
>
> Susan A., married George Dickerson ; she is dead.
>
> Herbert ; is dead.

Angeline (Denison) Trip's children :

> Frances, married and lives in Cortland, N. Y.

Wellington Denison's children :

> Frank, married and lives in Mich.
>
> Clayton, married and lives in Mich.
>
> Etta, married Lewis Dunning ; lives in Rome, N. Y.

12. Elihu Denison (son of Daniel Denison, Jr.),
born in Stephentown, N. Y., April 14, 1777. Was married
to Thankful Stewart about 1800, and settled in
Ohio. Their children are :

> Elihu ; Anna ; Thankful ; James ; Daniel ; Horace ;
> Katherine ; George, and Avery.

13. Thomas Denison (son of Daniel Denison, Jr.),
born May 5, 1779 ; was married Feb. 23, 1801, to
Polly Crary. They settled at Berne, Albany Co., N. Y.
Their children are :

> Thomas C., born Sept. 21, 1802 ; married Charity Schults;
> live at Hunt's Landing, Schoharie Co., N. Y.
>
> Mary, born April 30, 1804 ; married Ezra Orcut.
>
> Isaac, born July 21, 1806 ; married Mary Dibble.
>
> Katherine, born March 27, 1809 ; married Nathan Earl.
>
> Cadance, born July 14, 1811 ; married Ichabod Dibble.
>
> Daniel, born May 21, 1814 ; married Eliza Almy.
>
> Hannah, born Dec. 11, 1815 ; unmarried.
>
> Jesse W., born April 9, 1818 ; was married first in 1846,
> to Mary W. Briggs, and second in 1859, to Eliza B.
> Lewis. He was founder of the town of Denison,
> county seat of Crawford Co., Iowa, where he has lived
> for several years. He has five children : Mary Louisa ;
> Julia P. ; Willie S. ; Maria Louisa, and Jesse L.

THE SEVENTH GENERATION.

Record of Samuel Denison's Family.

Samuel Denison (son of Daniel Denison, Jr., and gr. gr. gr. gr. grandson of William Denison), was born at Stephentown, Rensselaer County, N. Y., Oct. 24, 1774. In 1800, he and his brother Latham migrated to the then great Western Wilderness, and settled upon adjoining farms in the town of Floyd, Oneida Co., N. Y. and each continued to own and occupy the farm so selected until his death. Floyd had then but few settlers, and those at remote points. It was his misfortune to be called upon to bear up under greater afflictions than usually befall the early settler. Just at the time he had so far subdued the forest as to make his farm yield an abundant support for himself and family, he accidentally pricked his right thigh with a pitchfork. The wound was apparently a slight one, and little attention was given to it at the time, but within a few days it became inflamed and painful, and after suffering intense anguish for several weeks, he was obliged to suffer amputation of his leg above the knee joint. The operation was performed by Dr. White, of Cooperstown, who was the nearest surgeon capable of performing such an operation, and to reach Floyd, he had to travel on horseback through the wilderness seventy-four miles. Added to this affliction of losing his leg, and the resulting confinement and sickness, his wife, who for a long time had been an invalid, died shortly after the amputation, leaving to be cared for seven young children, the eldest not over 17. During

all these misfortunes, afflictions, and sufferings, he
was hopeful, and his courage never failed him. I in-
sert the following tribute to his memory (as well as
that of other contemporary pioneers), taken from the
Rome *Sentinel*, of Dec. —, 1849. It was written by
the late Hon. Elon G. Comstock, who at the time was
editor of the *Sentinel*, and subsequently on the editorial
staff of the New York *Journal of Commerce :*

" Died in Floyd, on the 11th of December, 1849,
Samuel Denison, aged 76 years. Mr. Denison was one
of the early settlers of this county, having resided, we
think, on the same farm for almost half a century.
Although not the first, the town of Floyd was one of
the earliest settled towns in the county, but its pioneers,
many of whom have lived to good old age, are dropping
away, and a few years more will have removed all of
them from the scenes of their early adventures, and the
home of their manhood and old age. Mr. Denison
located in Floyd in the year 1800, or 49 years ago.
Several others came about the same time, a few prior
to his arrival, and others soon after ; but we regret that
we have not the information necessary to a correct account of the men and the occurrences of that early
period.

" Among the first settlers were Nathan Townsend,
James Chase, Nathaniel and William Allen, Latham
and Samuel Denison. Samuel Moulton and, we believe,
also the grandfather of Col. David Moulton, whose first
name we do not remember. There are, doubtless, several
others whose names will occur to those longer and
better acquainted with the early history of the town.
These settlements were made in different parts of the
town, while it was yet a wilderness, and while the

whole county was nearly in the same condition. There were settlements of several years' standing in Whitestown (by which name all the county north and west of Utica was then called), Fort Stanwix (now Rome), Western, Westmoreland, etc., but the population was sparse, and neighbors few and far between. It was at that day not unusual for citizens of Floyd to go with ox teams to Western, Lee, and other distant towns to meeting—a task which our present inhabitants would hardly feel willing to accomplish.

" Of the pioneer settlers named above, only two now remain. Mr. Salmon Moulton and Captain Townsend, the former still residing in Floyd, and the latter at Holland Patent, having retired from his farm several years ago. Mr. Chase died several years ago ; the two Allens about six years since, at an advanced age; and Mr. Latham Denison some four or five years ago. Mr. Samuel Denison, whose recent death has led to this brief and imperfect narrative, had continued to reside on the farm where he first located, and to enjoy the esteem and respect of his townsmen and acquaintances, until his death on Tuesday last. His health had for the past three or four years been seriously impaired, although such as to admit of the superintendence of the farm and business affairs. He was celebrated for his skill and intelligence with which he conducted his farm, and for many years has been a constant subscriber to agricultural papers, which he has perused with much interest, while those younger and less experienced have steadily rejected all such aid."

He was twice married—first to Rhoda Crandall, Jan. 13, 1802, by whom he had nine children. The wife, Rhoda, died Feb. 18, 1817.

The following are the children by his first wife :

1. Pamelia B., born Oct. 26, 1802 ; married Randall Spencer.
2. Alvin, born July 30, 1804; married Rhoda Eddy.
3. Catharine, born Nov. 19, 1805; married John T. G. Bailey.
4. Alson, born Aug. 12, 1807; died Nov. 19, 1808.
5. Sarah C., born June 22, 1809; married Hiram B. Reed.
6. Alexander H., born June 23, 1811; married Charlotte A. Huntly.
7. Alson, born Feb. 3, 1813; married Jane C. Goodno.
8. Lucy, born Feb. 27, 1815; died March 8, 1853; unmarried.
9. A child unnamed, born and died in 1817.

He was married the second time Dec. 28, 1817, to Nancy Burlingame, born March 3, 1798, daughter of Freeborn and Lydia (Bacon) Burlingame of Providence, R. I.

The children by this marriage are :

10. George B., born Feb. 13, 1819; married Margaret M. Lyon.
11. Charles M., born April 3, 1822; married Cornelia Pond.
12. Daniel A., born Feb. 7, 1824; died Feb. 1, 1838.
13. Rhoda, born March 15, 1826; married Harvey C. Martin.
14. Ellery, born Dec. 22, 1827; married Ellen K. Gibb.
15. Lydia E., born April 28, 1830 ; married J. W. Olds.
16. Clarissa E., born June 25, 1832; married James M. Colman.

He died Dec. 11, 1849, and was buried by the side of his first wife, Rhoda, in Floyd. His widow, Nancy, is now living at Vernon Centre, Oneida County, N. Y., in her 86th year ; strong and active, and writes a steadier hand than many people at 50.

THE EIGHTH GENERATION.

I.

Pamelia B. Denison's Family Record.

Pamelia B. Denison (daughter of Samuel Denison), born Oct. 26, 1802, was married to Randall Spencer, Jan'y 4, 1825. She died Oct. 8, 1837. We haven't the date of his death. They had these four children :

17. Harlow B., born Jan'y 21, 1826 ; died in infancy.
18. Catharine R., born Feb. 18, 1828 ; married Emery H. Card.
19. Ira M., born Dec. 5, 1829 ; married Sarah M. Wood.
20. Randall D., born April 14, 1833 ; married Susan Thurston.

GRANDCHILDREN OF PAMELIA.

18. Catharine Rhoda Spencer (daughter of Pamelia B.), born Feb. 18, 1828, was married to Emery H. Card, March 24, 1853. He was born Jan'y 9, 1829. He is an engineer on the N. Y., Ontario and Western R. R. They live at Norwich, Chenango Co., N. Y., and have three children.

21. Carrie P. Card, born March 9, 1855.
22. Hattie E. Card, born Sept. 3, 1863.
23. Freddie E. Card, born May 31, 1865.

---

19. Ira Milton Spencer (son of Pamelia B.), born Dec. 5, 1829, was married Dec. 7, 1848, to Sarah M. Wood, daughter of James and Patty Wood, born Jan'y 22, 1831. He is a farmer, and lives at Brookfield,

Madison Co., N. Y. He was a soldier in the Union Army. They have three children, and three grandchildren.

24. Randall Lee Mott Spencer, born Jan'y 5, 1850. Is
25. married and has one child (25), a girl. He is a physician, and lives in Trenton, Oneida Co., N. Y.
26. Delavan J. Spencer, born June 14, 1851, married Mary L. Coon. Lives at Roynsford Montgomery Co., Penn. They have two children.
27. Milton D. Spencer, born March 16, 1876.
28. Merton J. Spencer, born Aug. 22, 1877.
29. Sara De Etta Spencer, born Aug. 8, 1854. Unmarried, and lives in Utica, N. Y.

---

20. Randall D. Spencer (son of Pamelia B.), born April 14, 1833, was married Dec. 24, 1856, to Susan Thurston, daughter of Thomas and Elizabeth Thurston, of Woolverhampton, England. She was born April 10, 1833. He is a carpenter, and resides in Hamilton, Madison Co., N. Y. He was a soldier in the Union Army during the rebellion. They have one child and one grandchild.

30. Nellie Pamelia Spencer, born March 6, 1858. She married Rev. Charles P. P. Fox, March 6, 1876. He is a Baptist clergyman, and lives in Hamilton, N. Y. They have one child.
31. Herbert Spencer Fox, born May 13, 1879.

Yours truly
Ellery Denison M.D.

II.

Alvin Denison's Family Record.

Alvin Denison (son of Samuel Denison), born July 31, 1804, was married to Rhoda Eddy, Jan'y 18, 1827. She was born May 4, 1806. They lived in Floyd, where all their children were born. She died there Sept. 24, 1849. He died at his son's residence, in Ottawa, Ill., Dec. 11, 1881, and was taken to Floyd and buried by the side of his wife. They had seven children, as follows:

32. Abial S., born Nov. 28, 1828; married Philena J. Chubb.
33. Alburtus J., born March 27, 1831; married Mary E. Wilson.
34. Hiram E., born Feb. 18, 1833; died Feb. 3, 1875.
35. Ann J., born June 20, 1835; married Geo. W. Clark.
36. Horace A., born April 22, 1837; married Amelia A. Pate.
37. Catharine R., born Sept. 8, 1839; married Edmund K. Pierce.
38. Roxanna H., born Nov. 25, 1842; married Harrison H. Mitchell.

GRANDCHILDREN OF ALVIN'S.

32. Abial Samuel Denison (son of Alvin Denison), born Nov. 24, 1828, was married to Philena J. Chubb, Nov. 9, 1864. She was born in Sheffield, Loraine Co., Ohio, Dec. 11, 1834. They live at Baxter Springs, Cherokee Co., Kansas. They have had seven children.

39. Eva Denison, born Aug. 31, 1865; died June 13, 1866.
40. Clarence Denison, born June 23, 1866; died July 9, 1874.

2

41. Ralph Denison, born Feb. 22, 1868 ; died April 3, 1868.
42. Ernest Denison, born Dec. 4, 1869 ; died Oct. 3, 1873.
43. Nina Denison, born Feb. 28, 1872.
44. Samuel Eddy Denison, born Feb. 28, 1874.
45. Rhoda Denison, born July 30, 1876.

---

33. Alburtus J. Denison (son of Alvin Denison), born March 27, 1831, was married to Mary E. Wilson, Jan'y 9, 1856. She was born Nov. 11, 1836. His occupation is a merchant, and lives in Ottawa, Ill. They have eight children.

46. George Alvin, born Oct. 27, 1856.
47. Ida, born Feb. 22, 1861.
48. Rhoda Delta, born Aug. 8, 1863.
49. Ellsworth, born March 8, 1867.
50. Nettie, born Aug. 2, 1869.
51. Mary, born March 31, 1873.
52. Berten, born March 25, 1875.
53. Kittie, born June 5, 1878.

---

35. Ann Janette Denison (daughter of Alvin Denison), born June 30, 1835, was married to George W. Clark, March 7, 1855. He died in Nebraska, Oct. 15, 1858. She died in Kansas, March 16, 1870. They had two children.

54. Rhoda G., born Jan'y 25, 1857 ; died May 9, 1858.
55. George D., born Sept. 9, 1858 ; lives in Nebraska.

---

36. Horace Alvin Denison (son of Alvin Denison), born April 22, 1837, was married to Amelia A. Pate, May 8, 1864. She was born at Nashville, Washington Co., Ill., June 29, 1845. They live at Hoylton, Ill., and have three children.

56. Irene E., born July 6, 1866.
57. Cecil Alvin, born April 14, 1869.
58. Edith Amelia, born Aug. 23, 1880.

---

37. Catharine Rhoda Denison (daughter of Alvin Denison), born Sept. 8, 1839, was married to Edmund K. Pierce, Jan'y 25, 1859. They live on the homestead, in Floyd, Oneida Co., N. Y., and have these five children :

59. Franklin E. Pierce, born Sept. 25, 1860.
60. Rhoda Luella, born Oct. 4, 1862; died March 25, 1866.
61. Estelle, born Oct. 14, 1864.
62. Albert D., born Feb. 16, 1867.
63. Genevieve, born June 25, 1869.

---

38. Roxanna Hannah Denison (daughter of Alvin Denison). born Nov. 25, 1842, was married to Harrison H. Mitchell, Sept. 13, 1866. They reside in Syracuse, N. Y. No children.

III.

Catherine Denison (daughter of Samuel Denison), born Nov. 19, 1805, was married to John T. G. Baily, June 24, 1835. They reside in Brookfield, Madison County, N. Y. No children.

IV.

Alson Denison (son of Samuel Denison), born Aug. 12, 1807, died Nov. 19, 1808.

V.

Sarah C. Denison's Family Record.

Sarah C. Denison (daughter of Samuel Denison), born June 22, 1809, was married to Hiram B. Reed, May 21, 1829. He was born Oct. 31, 1805, in Chautauqua County, N. Y. She died April 27, 1863, and he died May 4, 1863. They were both buried in Hastings, Barry County, Mich. They had five children, as follows:

64. A son born at Rome, N. Y., Dec, 15, 1830 ; died same day.
65. Mary C., born at Rome, N. Y., Nov. 22, 1831 ; married Jared J. Bixby.
66. Emily E., born at Auburn, N. Y., March 29, 1837 ; twice married.
67. Charles H., born March 21, 1839; died May 19, 1868.
68. Milford C., born at Auburn, N. Y., June 1, 1841; married Angie Tyler.

Grandchildren of Sarah C. Denison.

65. Mary C. Reed (daughter of Sarah C.), born Nov. 22, 1831, was married to Jared J. Bixby, Oct. 16, 1851. He was born Oct. 24, 1831, and died at Utica, N. Y., March 28, 1881. She is now living at Poolville, Madison County, N. Y. They had these three children:

> **69.** Flora E., born Sept. 11, 1852; married Charles Markert; she died April 17, 1877.
>
> **70.** Henry C., born Oct. 17, 1854; married Mary A. Simmonds March 3, 1872; she was born Jan. 14, 1855; they have one child.
>
> **71.** Louie J. Simmonds, born Feb. 17, 1874.

----

66. Emily E. Reed (daughter of Sarah C.), born March 29, 1837, married first, Oscar F. Clark, of Unadilla Forks, N. Y., Jan. 2, 1854. He was born Dec. 14, 1834. They had:

> **72.** Charles E. Clark, born April 28, 1857; died March 9, 1860.
>
> **73.** George H., born Jan. 11, 1859; married Anna E. Griffith.
>
> **74.** Luna May, born Dec. 11, 1861; married Morgan Phillips.

Emily was married the second time to George S. Buell, June 20, 1866. They live in Buffalo, N. Y.

----

68. Milford Cody Reed (son of Sarah C.), born June 1, 1841, was married to Angie Tyler, May 2, 1871. Angie was born in Buffalo, N. Y., April 21, 1850. They have but one child:

> **75.** Nellie D., born at Buffalo, Feb. 15, 1872.

VI.

Alexander H. Denison's Family Record.

Alexander H. Denison (son of Samuel Denison), born June 23, 1811, was married to Charlotte A. Huntley, Aug. 17, 1836. She was born April 22, 1813. They live at Harrisburgh, Lewis County, N. Y. Their nine children are:

76. Beere L., born July 22, 1837; married Alice H. Peck.
77. Amelia A., born May 26, 1839; married David T. Williams.
78. Almon A., born Aug. 6, 1841; married Lucy Coffin.
79. Zilpha M., born March 17, 1844; died Feb. 10, 1859.
80. A son born and died May 23, 1847.
81. Emily G., born Oct. 1, 1848; died Feb. 2, 1859.
82. Harriet I., born July 14, 1852; married Brewster Young.
83. Angeline, born Jan. 16, 1854; died Aug. 2, 1872.
84. Frankie M., born Aug. 27, 1857; married Fred. Munger.

Grandchildren of Alexander :

76. Beere L. Denison (son of Alexander), born July 22, 1837, was married to Alice H. Peck, Dec. 15, 1869. She was born Jan. 8, 1851. He was a soldier in the Union Army. They live in Neosho, Mo. They have these children:

85. Alvin H., born at Jackson, Mich., Dec. 13, 1870.
86. Hattie A., born at Jackson, Mich., Aug. 30, 1873.
87. Jessie G. W., born in Neosho, Mo., Dec. 10, 1881.

----

77. Amelia A. Denison (daughter of Alexander), born May 26, 1839, married David T. Williams, Aug.

3, 1856. He was a soldier in the Union Army. They have one child:

89. Herbert Williams, born Nov. 21, 1863.

---

78. Almon A. Denison (son of Alexander), born Aug. 6, 1841, was married to Lucy Coffin, July 31, 1863. He was a soldier in the Union Army. They live at Port Leyden, Mich. He had these children by his first wife:

89. Minnie M., born March 9, 1869.
90. Lucy Edna, born Jan. 6, 1874.

The wife Lucy died, and he married Millie J. Goodenough, Oct. 14, 1874. The children by the second wife are:

91. Belle M., born Sept. 15, 1878.
92. Eva M., born Jan. 24, 1881.

---

82. Harriet I. Denison (daughter of Alexander), born July 14, 1852, married Brewster Young, Sept. 4, 1877. They have one child:

93. Benton I. Young, born Sept. 29, 1879.

---

84. Frankie M. Denison (daughter of Alexander), born Aug. 27, 1857, was married to Fred. Munger, May 26, 1880. Live in Kansas.

VII.

Alson Denison's Family Record.

Alson Denison (son of Samuel Denison), born Feb. 3, 1813, was married to Jane C. Goodno, Sept. 20, 1836. She was born Dec. 13, 1813. He now resides on his farm near Stanton, Montgomery County, Iowa. They have eight children :

94. Urbane A., born Sept. 19, 1838; married Georgie Ingersoll.

95. Lucy J., born June 5, 1840; married John F. Sims.

These two were born in Amboy, Oswego County, N. Y.

96. Clarissa A., born Oct. 25, 1843; married Theodore F. Worthington.

97. Furman H., born Sept. 5, 1846.

98. Samuel S., born Nov. 11, 1851.   Photographer.

These t   e were born in Camden, Oneida County, N. Y.

99. Julia L., born Aug. 13, 1854; married James F. Judkin.

100. Jessie F., born Dec. 11, 1856; married Charles D. Kellogg.

101. Emily A., born Oct. 29, 1859.

These three were born in Cambridge, Ill.

Alson's grandchildren :

94. Urbane A. Denison (son of Alson), born Sept. 19, 1838, was married to Georgie Ingersoll, Oct. 30, 1864. She was born in White Haven, Somerset County, Md., Jan. 7, 1842. He was a soldier in the Union Army ; was wounded in the shoulder, which

renders his arm useless, and has a clerkship in the
Pension Department at Washington, D. C. They have
two children :

102. Fenton Alson, born May 12, 1866.
103. Irving, born Jan. 5, 1880.

95. Lucy J. Denison (daughter of Alson), born June
5, 1840, married John F. Sims, in 1866. She died Dec.
13, 1871, and left one child, who lives with her grand-
parents.

104. Jesse Maud Sims, born March 4, 1867.

---

96. Clarissa A. Denison (daughter of Alson), born
Oct. 25, 1843, married Theodore F. Worthington, Sept.
4, 1862. He was born July 14, 1837. They reside in
Grinnell, Iowa. They have these children :

105. Mabel T. Worthington, born July 14, 1865.
106. Clarence E. Worthington, born Dec. 20, 1868.
107. Hattie L. Worthington, born Oct. 13, 1870.
108. Jessie F. Worthington, born Jan'y 29, 1873.
109. Carrol A. Worthington, born April 25, 1881.

---

99. Julia L. Denison (daughter of Alson), born
Aug. 13, 1854, married James F. Judkin, Oct. 19,
1879. He was born Jan'y 15, 1851. They live at
Grinnell, Iowa.

---

100. Jessie Fremont Denison (daughter of Alson),
born Dec. 11, 1856, was married to Charles D. Kellogg,
Aug. 30, 1880. They reside at Dixon, Ill.

2*

VIII.

Lucy Denison (daughter of Samuel Denison), born Feb. 27, 1815, died March 8th, 1853, unmarried.

IX.

A child, unnamed.

X.

George B. Denison's Family Record.

George B. Denison (son of Samuel Denison), born Feb. 13, 1819, was married to Margaret M. Lyon, Oct. 17, 1858. Margaret was a daughter of Dr. Benjamin Lyon, of Providence, R. I., and was born March 7, 1823, in the town of Russia, Herkimer Co., N. Y. He is a banker, and resides in Muscatine, Iowa, where their children were born. Their children are :

110. Charles O., born May 21, 1860 ; died June 18, 1861.
111. Emma, born Nov. 26, 1861 ; died June 13, 1863.
112. Edna, born Aug. 4, 1865.

XI.

Charles M. Denison's Family Record.

Charles M. Denison (son of Samuel Denison), born April 3, 1822, was married to Cornelia Pond, March 4, 1851, daughter of Julius Pond and July Ann Crary. He is a lawyer, resides at Whitesboro, Oneida Co., N. Y., and has an office in Utica. Was Assessor of Internal Revenue, 21st District, N. Y., from 1862 to 1870. Has held the office of Commissioner of the U. S. Circuit Court and Federal Chief Supervisor of Elections for the Northern District of N. Y. since 1872. In 1880 he was appointed by Governor Cornell a member of the Board of Canal Appraisers.

His children, all of whom were born in Rome, N. Y., are :

    113. Julia Crary, born May 25, 1852 ; died Aug. 4, 1852.
    114. George Ellery, born July 2, 1854 ; is a lawyer.
    115. John Whipple, born Aug. 25, 1859 ; died Aug. 26, 1860.
    116. Helen Hamilton, born Aug. 24, 1863 ; died Aug. 20, 1864.

XII.

Daniel A. Denison (son of Samuel Denison), born Feb. 7, 1824, died Feb. 1, 1838.

XIII.

Rhoda Denison's Family Record.

Rhoda Denison (daughter of Samuel Denison), born March 15, 1826, was married to Harvey C. Martin, Sept. 10, 1845, and lives at Vernon Center, Oneida Co., N. Y. Their children are :

117. Gilbert E. Martin, born Aug. 20, 1846 ; married Mary E. Church.
118. Ellery D., born Aug. 20, 1851 ; died June 25, 1854.
119. Fred. A., born June 20, 1854 ; married Alice Groff.
120. Lillie E., born April 1, 1856.
121. George B., born March 22, 1858 ; died July 10, 1858.
122. John M., born July 10, 1859.
123. Jessie Emma, born Feb. 4, 1863.

RHODA'S GRANDCHILDREN.

117. Gilbert E. Martin (son of Rhoda), born Aug. 20, 1846, married Mary E. Church, June 27, 1869. They live at Bear Lake, Warren Co., Penn., and have these children :

124. Millie Maud, born April 6, 1870.
125. Kenneth Merle, born July 3, 1881.

---

119. Fred. A. Martin (son of Rhoda), born June 20, 1854, married Alice Groff, Dec. 22, 1869. They have one child,

126. Son, born in Nov., 1880.

XIV.

Ellery Denison's Family Record.

Ellery Denison (son of Samuel Denison), born Dec. 22, 1827, married Ellen K. Gibb, May 20, 1857. She was born March 27, 1834. He is a physician and resides at 124 West 13th Street, New York. Their children are :

127. Charles Ellery, born Nov. 24, 1858 ; is a physician.
128. Emma Kezia, born Aug. 27, 1860.
129. George Burlingame, born Dec. 28, 1863 ; died Oct. 28, 1869.
130. Henry Avery, born Oct. 22, 1866; died Feb. 7, 1869.
131. Edward Gibb, born April 5, 1871 ; died Aug. 4, 1871.
132. William Samuel, born Oct. 23, 1873.
133. Ellen Louise, born Sept. 26, 1878.

XV.

Lydia E. Denison's Family Record.

Lydia E. Denison (daughter of Samuel Denison), born April 28, 1830, was married to J. Whitney Olds, Jan'y 2, 1856. She died July 1, 1881, in Chicago, Ill., and was buried at Rose Hill Cemetery. They had these two children:

134. Charles W. Olds, born Dec. 4, 1856.
135. George D. Olds, born Jan'y 6, 1861.

XVI.

Clarissa E. Denison's Family Record.

Clarissa E. Denison (daughter of Samuel Denison), born June 25, 1832, was married in Muscatine, Iowa, Feb. 15, 1859, to James M. Colman, from Providence, R. I. They first lived in Hartford City, West Virginia; after the close of the civil war they moved to Brunswick, Georgia, where they resided for several years. Afterward they removed to Savannah, Ga., where he held a position in the Custom House. They now reside at Seattle, Washington T'y. They have these children :

136. Mary, born Dec. 15, 1859 ; married Wm. H. Hutchinson, Jan'y 1, 1883.
137. James M., born Sept. 6, 1862.
138. Clara June, born June 1, 1865.

These three were born in Hartford City, West Va.

139. George Lathrop, born in Brunswick, Ga., April 23, 1872.

CAPT. GEORGE DENISON.

CAPT. GEORGE DENISON, emigrant, the head of the clan whose family records are given in this genealogy, came over to this country in the good ship *Lion*, with his father, William Denison, his brothers Daniel and Edward, and Rev. John Eliot, the apostle to the Indians. George was at this time thirteen years of age, and, doubtless, received much of his mental and moral training from Mr. Eliot, who was tutor in his father's family. William Denison was a merchant, and from the fact that he employed a tutor in his family, it is inferred that he must have been a man of considerable means. He was a deacon in the First Church in Roxbury, Conn., a man of liberal education, and of large influence in the colony.

His wife did not come to this country until 1632, and did not unite with the Church until some years later.

William Denison built a house in Roxbury, and it remains until this day in good preservation. He died there, Jan. 25, 1653, an old man. She died there Feb. 23, 1645.

George Denison began his adult life in Roxbury, and at the age of 22 married Bridget Thompson in 1640. She was the daughter of John Thompson, gentleman, of Preston, Northamptonshire, England, whose widow, Alice, had come to America, and was living in Roxbury. We find quite widely distributed among the descendants a courtship letter in verse, addressed by our ancestor to Miss Bridget Thompson, who seems to have been his first flame. We make room for it, not only as an interesting relic of the olden time, and a sample of the methods of courtship in 1640, but to correct a little romance, invented by one of his descendants, which alleges that he was betrothed to Ann Borodell before he came to this country, and hastened back to her immediately upon the death of his first wife.

There is no evidence of this, but much to the contrary. He was but thirteen when he emigrated, and probably never heard of Ann Borodell until he was carried a wounded soldier to her father's house, John Borodell, of Cork, Ireland (who was then living in England), where Ann became his nurse, and afterward his wife. Whatever we may think of the literary merit of these verses, they seem to have prevailed with Miss Bridget :

CAPT. GEORGE DENISON'S COURTSHIP LETTER TO BRIDGET THOMPSON.

It is an ordinance, my dear, divine,
Which God unto the sons of men makes shine,
Even marriage, to that whereof I speak,
And unto you therein my mind I break.

In Paradise, oft Adam God did tell
To be alone for man would not be well;
He in his wisdom, therefore, thought it right
To bring a woman into Adam's sight.

A helper that for him might be most meet,
To comfort him by her doing discreet.
I of that stock am sprung—I mean from him—
And also of that tree I am a limb.

A branch, tho' young, yet I do think it good
That God's great vow by man be not withstood ;
Alone I am, a helper I would find,
That might give satisfaction to my mind.

The party that doth satisfy the same
Is Miss Bridget Thompson by her name ;
God having drawn my affections unto thee,
My heart's desire is that thine may be to me.

This, with my blottings—tho' they trouble you,
Yet pass them by, because I know not how—
Though they at this time should much better be,
For love it is that first has been to thee.

And I would wish that they much better were;
Therefore, I pray, accept them as they are;
So hoping my desire I shall obtain,
Your own true love,

A.D. 1640.   GEORGE DENISON, by name.

After three years of wedded life, Bridget died, leaving two daughters, Sarah and Hannah, who lived to be the heads of families in Stonington. Very soon after her death he returned to England, enlisted under Cromwell in the army of the Parliament, won distinction, was wounded at Naseby, was nursed at the house of John Borodell by his daughter Ann, which led to his marriage with her, and his early return to Roxbury, where he was chosen captain, and was called "a young soldier lately come out of the wars in England." He is said to have had one son, John, born July 14, 1646, when he came to Roxbury the second time, which would make his absence about three years.

He did not long content himself with the quiet life in Roxbury. His daughter Ann had been born to him in that place, May 20, 1649. In 1651, he left Roxbury with his wife and four children for the Pequot settlement upon the west bank of the Thames, now New London. Here he had a house and lot given him by the town, which he occupied until 1654, when he sold out, went to Stonington, and settled on the land, a part of which has been in the possession of his descendants until the present generation, a tract of some five hundred acres in all, lying east of Pequotsop brook. His homestead place was bounded on the west by John Stanton's farm, now mainly owned by Joseph S. Williams; on the south by the Mason highway, which, with slight variations, is the road from Mystic Bridge to the Road Church, eastward to Palmer hill, and then by Amos Richardson's land, easterly by Richardson's land and the town lots, and westerly by said lots and lands of Capt. John Gallup.

The first house was probably a log house, which only served a temporary purpose, and was removed in Captain Denison's lifetime to make room for his mansion house. This was located in the northwest corner of his tract, a few feet west of the present dwelling of the Misses Sarah and Phebe M. Denison.

The spot was undoubtedly selected, with the eye of a military leader, for the purpose of defense against Indians, who were then numerous and disputed possession of the country with the English.

There is no other spot so eligible for the purpose of defense in the neighborhood.

The house stood upon the southern slope of a narrow plot of ground about twenty-five rods long, buttressed with steep ledges on every side. This acre of ground, more or less, elevated from twenty to thirty feet above the surrounding ravines, and stockaded, was impregnable against any force the Indians could muster. There was a stone fort inside of the stockade near the house, and the remains of the old wall are still pointed out.

It was removed about a hundred years ago by those who had slight appreciation of the value of historical monuments. The stones are still visible in the walls near the house. The location is a pleasant one, standing high above the adjacent fields and looking out southward over a broad tract of intervale, once probably cultivated by the aborigines, and now lying in meadow, the best part of the neighboring farms.

In this direction you get glimpses of the Mystic River and the Sound, with Fisher's Island and Long Island in the distance. To the west lies Pequod hill, once crowned with an Indian fort, and the scene of the terrible slaughter under Capt. John Mason. To the north lies Quocataug, with the Mystic valley on the left, stretching away toward Lantern hill—a scene of rural beauty not easily matched in the county. The land has many ledges, with loose well rounded bowlders upon the top, left in the ice period, geologists tell us, and ground into their present form by the moving glaciers. It is still hard land, even for Stonington, with rough pastures which the plow has never broken and probably never will. There are, however, smooth fertile acres between. Emigrants had been here five years before Captain Denison, to spy out the land, and the best locations had already been appropriated.

The mansion house which he erected could not have been a very imposing or substantial structure, for it was removed by his grandson George, son of William, about the year of 1724. Tradition affirms that George, eldest son of George and Lucy Gallup Denison, was

the first child born in the new house. The records fix
the date of his birth July 9, 1725, and that of his next
older sister, Mary, July 14, 1724. This would make
the age of the present structure 160 years, in the present year 1884. Upon this spot seven generations of the
Denison family have been born. William[2] was probably born in the log house ; his son, George,[3] was born
in the mansion house ; his son, George,[4] Oliver,[5] Oliver,[6] Edgar,[7] and his children. The present farm of
250 acres remained undivided from George[3] until the
death of the sixth owner, Oliver,[6] in the year 1873, a
period of two hundred and twenty years from the settlement. About fifty acres, including the house and
outbuildings, were deeded to his daughters, Sarah and
Phebe, and the rest of the land divided among the other
heirs. It is quite rare in this country to find a farm
that has been held in the same family by inheritance
for seven generations.

Perched on this ledge of rocks, like a baron in his
castle, Captain Denison had a commanding influence
among his townsmen for forty years, was their trusted
military leader in forays against the Indians, and their
frequent representative at the General Court at Hartford.
He had great executive ability, and managed well the
public trusts committed to him, and his own private
affairs. He not only lived and raised a numerous
family from these rude acres, but accumulated, for those
times, a large estate. Numerous tracts of land were
given to him by the authorities, for his military service
principally, so that at the time of his death he owned
several thousand acres of land in Stonington, in Norwich and Windham, and in the State of Rhode Island.
This laid the foundation of comfortable homes for his

children and their descendants for several generations, and retained nearly all of them within easy reach of the ancestral homestead for a hundred years after his death.

His sons and his daughters, with the exception of Margaret, who went to Swanzey, Mass., all remained in Stonington, or in adjoining towns. Of his eleven grandsons four remained in Stonington, two in Westerly, R. I., one in North Stonington, one in Montville, one in New London, and two in Saybrook. Nearly all were quite large landholders and men of influence in their respective towns.

It is a little remarkable that none of the sons or grandsons, with a single exception, obtained the good old age of the emigrants. Capt. Denison died at the age of 76, and his wife, Ann Borodell, at 97, which shows that our emigrant ancestors were favored with unusual physical vigor. Of their three sons, John died at 52, and George and William at 59. William only survived his mother a year and a half. The grandsons died at the ages of 30, 37, 38, 40, 43, 46, 55, 64, 67, 86. This last was George, the son of William, who lived at Pequotsop, and removed the mansion house to make room for the present more spacious dwelling. The hardships of the wilderness will hardly account for this diminution of vital force in the second and third generations. They were almost all cut off in the midst of life ; and they had fewer difficulties and less exposure than the emigrants. It is not improbable that the products of the orchards they planted and the barley they harvested, when manufactured into alcoholic beverages, proved more perilous to life than struggles with the primitive forest and the Indians.

Later generations seem to have recovered the vigor of the founders of the clan, and give us a long list of persons who passed their three-score years and ten. There is food for profitable reflection in these statistics.

There is a solitary entry upon the records of the First Church of Stonington, under date of August 24, 1684 : "Capt. Denison was took into full communion," which shows that his mind had not been much occupied with religious things until late in life. The name of his wife appears among the communicants at the organization of the church, ten years earlier.

His active military life, and the clearing of the wilderness had not favored religious culture. His will, made ten years later, shows a very positive religious character, and a warm appreciation of his pastor, Rev. James Noyes, and of "the well bringing up and educating his grandchildren in religion and good learning."

The selection of the youngest son to be the principal heir, and to take the homestead, is probably a practical protest against the aristocratic usage of the mother country, which makes the eldest the favorite.

William, the youngest son of Capt. Denison, takes the homestead and cares for his widowed mother. The youngest sons of John, George, and William also inherit the homestead of the respective fathers.

The descendants of Capt. Denison began to swarm from the hive in the fourth generation, and are now to be found in almost all States of the Union, and in Nova Scotia and Canada. Capt. Robert Denison, son of Robert, of Mohegan, was of the fourth generation, settled in Nova Scotia, and has a numerous and highly respectable posterity in that province.

Robert Denison, of the fifth generation, son of Daniel, emigrated to Knox, N. Y., and from there two of his sons and three of his daughters went to Napanee, Ontario, Canada, and became the founders of the Canada branch of the family. There was a large emigration, quite early, to Vermont and border towns in Massachusetts, and about the same time or a little later, to New York and Pennsylvania. Thence they have spread westward, to Ohio and the Northwestern States, across the continent to California and Oregon. Only a few have reported from the Southern States.

The intermarriage of Capt. Denison's daughters and grand-daughters with the Palmers, Cheseboros, Stantons, Williamses, Billingses, Browns, and Babcocks, gives him a very numerous posterity in Stonington and vicinity. Nearly half the people of the town can trace their lineage back to Capt. Denison. It is only incidentally that we have traced the descendants of the Denison women beyond their own children. If this were to be done, down to the present generation, it would make another volume as large as the present. If this should ever happen, it will be undertaken by some person who has faint conception of the patience and labor it involves.

Of his wife, Ann Borodell, daughter of John Borodell, of Cork, Ireland, it is agreed by all the traditions that have come down to us in the several branches of her descendants, that she was remarkable for her fine personal appearance and lady-like manners. On account of these qualities she was commonly called "Lady Ann," which was a much higher compliment than

Yours truly
C M Denison

to have inherited the title. This has been claimed for her, but without authority. In some branches of the family there are fine samples of embroidery, which show her skill in needle-work. The widow of the late Isaac D. Miner, of Mystic Bridge, Conn., has one of these samples with an authentic record handed down through seven generations. It is still in good preservation.

Mrs. Charles T. Stanton, of Stonington, has a case of drawers, once her property, and given by her to her daughter, Borodell, who married Samuel Stanton. There are other relics of Lady Ann at the old homestead where she once ruled. She had a brother John Borodell, who came to this country and settled; also a sister Margaret, who married a Shepherd, and for whom her daughter Margaret was probably named. This sister had descendants, one of whom married a Wheeler; and Joseph Noyes, who married Zurviah Wheeler, has a descendant of Margaret Borodell Shepherd for his wife. Ann Borodell must have been well born, for she lived amid the hardships of pioneer life to the remarkable age of 97. The remains were disinterred some twenty years ago and removed from the old burying-ground, at the foot of Denison Street, to the Denison plot in the Elm Grove Cemetery. Here a substantial granite monument was erected to the memory of her husband about thirty years ago by contributions from his descendants. Deacon Ebenezer Denison, Senior, was the principal mover in this filial work, and it was among the last of the many good deeds of his life.

The following account of the main incidents of his life is given by Richard A. Wheeler, in his history of the First Church of Stonington:

"Captain Denison took an active and decided part

3

in 1656, in favor of having 'Mystic and Pawcatuck' set off, and a new township with a ministry of its own established. By this course he incurred the displeasure of the leading men of Pequot, and by favoring the claims of Massachusetts to the jurisdiction of the place, he drew upon himself the censure of the General Court, and when Southerton was incorporated and annexed to Suffolk County he was appointed first townsman, commissioner, and 'clerk of the writs.' He was active and influential in securing the favor of the Massachusetts Court, and aided in securing large grants of land here to parties there, which overlapped grants made to Cheseborough, Stanton, Palmer, and others by the General Court of Connecticut. This alienated some of his friends. But the reunion of the settlement by means of the new charter had the effect of extinguishing these Massachusetts claims, and the Connecticut grants were left undisturbed.

" When Mr. Cheseborough, in 1664, asked the General Court of Connecticut for amnesty for the planters who had favored the claim of Massachusetts to this place, it was readily granted for all except Captain Denison. Two years later it was extended to him, and ever afterward he was regarded with favor by the General Court.

" From 1671 to 1694 he represented Stonington for fifteen sessions of the General Court. He was appointed magistrate, selectman, and held almost every office in town.

" While Captain Denison was prominent and active in civil affairs, he was more distinguished in military matters. With the exception of Captain John Mason, he was the most conspicuous and daring soldier of New

London County, a natural military leader, and though holding the rank of captain, he often commanded expeditions against the Indians, and was always most successful when commander-in-chief. He participated in the Narragansett Swamp fight in 1675, and performed prodigies of valor. As early as February following that event a series of forays were commenced against the Narragansett Indians. They were commanded by Captain Denison and Captain James Avery. These partisan bands were composed of volunteers, regular soldiers, Pequots, Mohegans, and Nianties. It was the third of these roving excursions, begun in March and ended April 10, 1676, in which the celebrated Narragansett chieftain, Canochet, was taken prisoner. He was brought to Stonington, and put to death at Anguilla, near where Gideon P. Chesebro now resides. A council of war was held, during which his life was promised him if he would use his influence with the Indians to put a stop to the war, but he indignantly refused, saying that the Indians would not yield on any terms.

"He was told of his breach of faith in not keeping the treaties which he had made with the English, and of the men, women, and children he had massacred, and how he had threatened to burn the English in their houses; to all of which he haughtily and briefly replied, 'that he was now in their hands, and they could do with him as they pleased.' He was importuned and urged to let a councillor of his go and treat with his people, but he haughtily refused, whereupon the council of war voted for his immediate execution.

"When Canochet was told that he must die, he seemed not at all moved, but said, 'that he liked it well, and that he should die before his heart had grown soft, or he had said anything unworthy of himself.' He was shot by Oneco, son of Uncas, and by Cassasinnamon and Herman Garrett, two Pequot sachems.

"The Mohegans quartered him, and the Niantics built a fire and burned his remains. His head was sent as 'a token of love' to the Council at Hartford.

"In June following, Captain Denison commanded a company raised in New London County, for Major Talcott's expedition against the Indians in Massachusetts. They went as far north as Northampton, and returned after having scoured the country far up the Connecticut River, but met with a very few of the Indians. After a few days' rest the army went again in pursuit of the Indians. This time they went first to the northwest of Providence, then south to Point Judith, then home through Westerly and Stonington to New London.

"After a short respite, they started again, July 18, 1676, and made their way this time into Plymouth Colony. They went to Taunton, from whence they returned homeward, but hearing that a large number of Indians were working their way westward, making depredations as they went, they pursued and overtook them, and had a sharp and final struggle with them beyond the Housatonic, after which they returned, and the men were disbanded.

"There were ten of these expeditions, including the volunteer forays, under Denison and Avery. They inflicted speedy vengeance upon the Indians, and broke their power forever. The remnants of the Indian tribes were gathered together, and located wherever the English desired. In all these military expeditions Captain Denison bore a conspicuous part, and won for himself undying fame."

CAPT. JOHN DENISON.

It seems strange that so little should be known among his descendants, of a man so conspicuous in his time as Capt. John Denison. He was the first born of Capt. George Denison and his wife, Ann Borodell, married to Phebe Lay, Nov. 26, 1667, at the age of 21, after each party had been duly apportioned by their fathers in a legal contract recorded at Saybrook. They were blessed with nine children, six sons and three daughters, of whom one died in infancy. All the rest lived to be married, and with a single exception, had large families and numerous posterity. Large tracts of land were given to each of the sons, generally during the father's lifetime. And yet there were no stones for his grave, or that of his wife, and it was a long time before we found the place of their burial. A genealogy of the Chesebro' and Denison families, kept by Daniel Chesebro', who lived near the head of the river, incidentally states that they were buried in the burying-ground at the foot of Denison street, in the village of Mystic Bridge. We had looked diligently for these graves in Saybrook, near the village of Essex, where his eldest son, John, settled upon the farm given to them by Robert Lay, but no trace of a grave or stone was to be found there, nor of his son John, nor of his grandsons Daniel and John, who died there. There is a stone at the grave of his grandson James, who died before marriage, and of his grandson Jabez, who had a large family, and died at the age of 90. In those early times gravestones were brought from England, and the building of monuments was so expensive that many of

the early settlers' graves were marked by no headstones
that had inscriptions.

His five sons were all men of influence, and left
families.   His descendants numbered in the book are
3,374. Those of his brothers William and George, com-
bined, only numbered 2,405 so far as they are recorded.
His son John died at the early age of 30, soon after his
settlement in Saybrook, leaving five children, the
youngest, Jabez, being but six months old. The second
son, George, received a liberal education at Harvard
College, was settled as a lawyer at New London, and
was for a time clerk of the County Court.   Robert
settled in Mohegan, near Gardner's lake, now Montville,
was a large land holder by purchase from the Indians,
was among the founders of the church there, was twice
married, and had twelve children by his first wife and
two by the second.

William, the fourth son, settled in the northwest
corner of Stonington, now North Stonington, upon
land owned by his grandfather, Capt. George, and inherited from his father.   It remained in the family
several generations.

He had twelve children, and was the progenitor of
one of the most prolific and enterprising branches of
the family.

Descendants are still very numerous in Stonington,
though the homestead has passed out of the family.
Still more are found in New York State, in Vermont
and in Maine. Daniel, the youngest son, remained upon
the homestead in what is now the village of Mystic
Bridge, and reared a numerous family.   The old Denison house was probably built by Capt. John.

It is mentioned in the diary of Thomas Miner, a contemporary, as being moved a short time before his death. How long it had stood before the moving we have no means of knowing. It is a venerable pile, probably the oldest house in town ; nearly or quite two hundred years old. The farm originally embraced all the land lying south of the Westerly road and west of Pequotsop brook, extending to the river on the west and south. In this old house six generations of Capt. John's descendants have been born and brought up. The shingles upon the east side are said to be as old as the building. It is now quite out of repair and used as a tenement house. The timbers in it are large and sound, and might last many years if the building were kept in repair.

The items from the inventory which accompanies the will are interesting, as they show the state of society and the simplicity of the early days. The wearing apparel of the lady of the house is appraised at £15, which, though it may seem small now, represented then a goodly display of " woman's clothes," on Sunday at the Road meeting-house, the only church building in town.

Meager as this is, £6 is still smaller allowance for the " wearing clothes " of Capt. Denison. Their mode of travel is indicated by the generous supply of horse-flesh, " 2 horses, 2 mares and 4 3-years-old colts."

There were no carriages or four-wheeled vehicles of any kind in those days for pleasure rides. The ambition of the thrifty settlers was to have a horse or colt for each son and daughter to ride as they grew up.

The roads were rough and hardly suitable for modern vehicles. There was comparatively little travel between Sundays, and most of the people, in-doors and out, were busy with the hard problem of sustaining life. It was the age of homespun, and the women had their hands full in carding, spinning, weaving and bleaching every yard of cloth that was to be manufactured into clothing for the family.

Sunday was the great day of the week for the family display, as well as for worship.

The descendants of Capt. John who have a lively imagination can picture the scene as the seven steeds, saddled and bridled, were brought up to the horse-block on Sunday morning, and one after another the parents and children mounted, and took the east road over the hills toward the meeting-house, to hear a discourse from that learned and godly man Rev. James Noyes. The sanctuary was the chief place of concourse, the center of news, and had to answer most of the ends of the newspapers and magazines of various sorts. The amount of time devoted to reading in the family, can readily be guessed from that item in the inventory, "a bible and other books and a brush, 10 shillings." This very small sum covered all the accumulations of reading matter in a married life of thirty years. The gold ring, £2 12s., was five times more valuable than all the books in the house. This ring possibly was the gift of Phebe to Capt. John when he went wooing in the early days to Saybrook. It ought to be in existence at this day among some of his descendants. Who will produce it?

MAJOR-GENERAL DANIEL DENISON.

For one who was so conspicuous in the early history of the colony of Massachusetts Bay as Major-General Daniel Denison, there is little left upon record. We glean the following from an article in the " Genealogical Register of New England," by Dr. Daniel Denison Slade of Boston, published in 1869.

" There is much uncertainty as to the origin of the family name. It is variously spelt Denison, Dennison, Denyson, Dennistown. It is unquestionably of ancient and probably of Norman origin. In the " Patronymia Britannica " is the following notice : ' The Dennistowns ' of that ilk have an extraordinary way of accounting for their surname. * One Danziel, or Daniel (say they), probably of Norman extraction, settled in Renfrewshire, and, calling the estate Danzielstown, assumed therefrom his surname. The family are unquestionably ancient, the name appearing in the Charter of King Malcolm I., who died in 1165, but the Norman Danziel is probably a fiction. The English Denisons are said to have sprung from a cadet of this ancient house, who went from Scotland in the time of Charles I., who fought at Marston Moor."

Daniel, the oldest son of William and Margaret Denison, was born in England in 1612, and came to this country probably in the ship Lion in 1631, with his

---

* Burke's " Book of the Landed Gentry of Great Britain " gives this as true, and says the Norman's name was " Danziel." He called his place " Danzielstoun " and from this came Denison. He was a full-blooded Norman.

3*

father, and brothers Edward and George, the Winthrops,
and Rev. John Eliot being his fellow voyagers. Daniel
was then nineteen years old. The following year, 1632,
he removed from Roxbury to Newtown (Cambridge),
his name being on the list of first settlers and church
members. He there married Patience, the daughter of
Gov. Thomas Dudley, who was at this time a resident
of the place. At a general court holden "att Newtown,
March 4, 1634," Mr. Denison was appointed to assist in
setting out " the bounds of ground betweene Newtowne
and Rocksberry." He took the oath of freeman, April
1st, 1634 ; and under the same date, the court grant
him two hundred acres, "all lying and being about the
ffalls, easterly side of Charles River."

With eight others, he is authorized by a general
Court at Newtowne, Sept. 3, 1634, to " sett out the
bounds of all towns not yet sett out, and to settle all
differences between any towns." He is also, with N.
Easton, to have charge of powder at Ipswich, which is
the first allusion we find to his military predilections.

In the following year, land was assigned to him in
Ipswich, with " a house lot of about two acres, which
he hath paled in, and built a house upon." To this
plantation he at once removed, and with its history his
name is closely united during the remainder of his
days. It is difficult to conceive why, after having con-
nected himself with the church and town affairs of
Cambridge, he should so soon have quitted them for
another abode. The probability, however, is that the
uncertainties which attended the project of establishing
the capital at Newtowne, and the differences which in
this matter sprung up between Gov. Winthrop and his
father-in-law, Mr. Dudley, whose cause he would nat-

urally espouse, and who removed to Ipswich in 1635, decided him to take this step. Whatever may have been the reasons for the course pursued, Mr. Denison at once commenced his public career of usefulness and honor in his new home. During the first year of his residence in Ipswich he was returned as deputy, in which capacity he served for three consecutive years, from 1635 to 1638. He was again elected in 1640, '44, '48, '49, '51 'and '52. As a member of the memorable court of November, 1637, he ordered those who had sympathized with Mrs. Hutchinson and Mr. Wheelwright to be disarmed, and among these were his father and brother, " their arms to be delivered to Gov. Johnson."

In 1636 he was made town clerk of Ipswich, " to have sixpence for every entrance of land." In the same year, by the General Court he is chosen captain of Ipswich ; with twelve others, he is deputed to assign the amount due from each town toward a sum to be levied for public uses. A quarterly Court having in 1636 been ordered to sit in Ipswich, Capt. Daniel Denison and Mr. Samuel Apleton were chosen to assist in these courts. Thus within the space of two years after becoming a resident of Ipswich, we find Mr. Denison serving his countrymen in offices pertaining to town affairs, and to those of the colony, as well as in a military capacity.

Sept. 6, 1638, Capt. Denison, with Mr. Bradstreet and ten others, was allowed upon their petition, " to begin a plantation at Merrimack," and to have " liberty to associate to them such others as they can agree upon." At the same session of the court he was appointed with fifteen others, " to consider of the manner and time of payment of a rate of £1200, and to lay it upon every towne pportionably" to be paid "at two months."

In 1641, he was one of a committee for furthering the trade of Ipswich. They were "to set up buoys, beacons, provide salt, cotton sowing hempseed, flaxseed and card wire." The town granted him, in 1643, 200 acres of land, "for his better encouragement to settle among us."

Great alarm having spread through the colonies, from a report that a general conspiracy existed among the native tribes, of which Miantonomo, the chief of the Narragansetts, was a principal instigator, a general training of troops and provision of arms were ordered, and Capt. Denison, with five others, was authorized at a session of the General Court, May 10, 1643, to put the country into a posture of war, and to see to fortifications.

On petition, several gentlemen of Ipswich, Beverly, and the adjoining towns, among whom was Capt. Denison, "out of care for the safety of the public weal, by the advancement of the military art and exercise of arms," were incorporated as a military company. The inhabitants of Ipswich agree to pay him £24 7s. annually as their military leader. In the year preceding, he had been chosen sergeant-major, which office he held until his election as major-general. Johnson, in his "*Wonder-working Providence*," thus speaks of him: "The two counties of Essex and Norfolk are for present joyned in one regiment; their first major who now commandeth this regiment is the proper and valient Major General Daniel Denison, a good soldier and of a quick capacity, not inferiour to any of these other chief officers : his own company are well instructed in feats of warlike activity."

The House of Representatives conferred the honor of speakership upon him during the two sessions of 1649, and again in the years 1651 and 1652. Mindful of the great importance of education and of the interests of his town, Major Denison was instrumental in establishing the grammar school of Ipswich, and was made one of the ffeoffers in 1651. He afterward gave freely for its maintenance. In 1651 he petitioned the General Court to confirm a grant of 267 acres, which had been assigned to his father, " and in consideration of the said grant and their favor to mee, they be pleased to grant to mee and my heirs forever 600 acres of land, where it may be found, according to law." After several years, the court granted his request, but the land was not laid out until July, 1662.

In the following year he was ordered to supply the place of Gen. Robert Sedgwick, who was absent. To the office of major-general he was appointed in 1653, and held it at different times until 1680. In this year he was chosen an Assistant, and thenceforward to his decease. In September he was elected Secretary of the Colony, in the absence of Edward Rawson. In May General Denison was appointed by the court one of a committee to join with the commissioners of the United Colonies to draw up the case respecting the " Dutch and Indians." A few years previous he had been placed on a committee, with the governor and two others, "for the purpose of ending differences, settling trade, &c., with the Dutch." Not coming to any agreement, Mr. Eaton, on the part of the commissioners, and Major Denison, on the part of the General

Court, were instructed to prepare, each of them, a short draft to be presented to the court and elders. While Eaton was "clamorous for war." Denison did not advocate extreme measures, and it was undoubtedly greatly through his influence that the House of Deputies communicated to the commissioners their resolve "that according to their best apprehensions in the case they doe not understand wee are caled to make a present warr with the Dutch."

In the spring of this year intelligence was brought that thousands of Indians had assembled at Piscataqua. Accordingly General Denison ordered out a scouting party of twenty-seven men, "to make a true discovery, and to quiet the minds of the inhabitants, who were much distracted and taken of their employments." They were absent on service from Friday morning until Monday night, and were allowed as pay, for each private one shilling, and two troopers two shillings and six pence per day. The alarm was without foundation.

He was appointed, with three others, to keep the county courts at Salisbury and Hampton. In May, 1654, a committee of three was chosen, of which General Denison was one, "to examine, compare, reconcile, and place together, in good order, all former laws, both printed and written." Whether the committee performed this labor or not, is uncertain. At any rate, the following order was passed by the General Court four years afterward, May 26, 1658: "That Major General Daniel Denison diligently peruse, examine, and weigh every law, and compare them with others of like nature; and such as are clear, plain, and good, free from any just exception, to stand without any animadversion as approved. Such as are repealed, or fit to be repealed, to be so marked, and the reason given; such as are obscure, contradictory, or seeming so, to be rectified, and the emendations prepared. When there is two or more laws about one and the same thing, to prepare a draught of one law, that may comprehend the same; to make a plain and easy table, and to prepare what else may present, in the perusing of them, to be necessary and useful, and make return at the next session of this court." The general entered upon this work with zeal, and in a few months produced the volume, which was at once printed. Two copies of the volume are still in existence. As compensation "for his great paines in transcribing the laws," the court granted him "a quarter part of Block Island;" the remaining portions were granted to Endicott, Bellingham, and Hathorne. These in turn sold the island to John Alcock for the sum of £400, in 1660.

During the next month, by order of the court, he met Mr. Bradstreet and Mr. Symonds, at Ipswich, "about a narrative in way of remonstrance of all matters respecting that which is charged on the General Court concerning the breach of the confederacy, for the vindication of this court's actions in such respects." This meeting was in reference to recent dissensions in the confederacy, in which Massachusetts had, by her course of action, been accused by the other colonies of breaking the covenant. This narrative, together with answers to a letter received from the Lord Protector, were to be sent to Cromwell.

In 1655 he was on a committee appointed for the county of Essex, "for the procuring of suitable supplies," and "to consider of some such way as whereby both merchandizing may be encouraged, and the hands also of the husbandman may not wax weary in his employment."

Massachusetts, considering that she had a prior right to certain territory on the northeast, claimed by representative of Gorges & Rigby, the court, at its session, October, 1657, appointed Gen. Denison, with Mr. Bradstreet and Mr. Hathorne, as commissioners to proceed to Kittery, and to confer with the inhabitants, who were dissatisfied with the existing state of affairs under which they lived. After long delay, and much consideration, Kittery submitted to the jurisdiction of Massachusetts. The commissioners next proceeded to Agamenticus (afterward York), and to other places, which were received on the same terms as Kittery.

As one of the confederate commissioners, to which office he was called in 1654, and in which he served faithfully until 1663, he addressing a letter to the Governor of Rhode Island, respecting the Quakers : " We therefore make it our request, that you, as the rest of the colonies, take such order herein that your neighbors may be freed from that danger ; that you remove those Quakers that have been received, and for the future prohibit their coming among you. We further declare that we apprehend that it will be our duty seriously to consider what further provision God may call us to make to prevent the aforesaid mischief."

As commissioner, with Mr. Bradstreet he dissented from the message and instructions given by their fellow commissioners of the other colonies, to his brother, Capt. George Denison, and two others, by which they were to go to Ninigret, the Niantic sachem, and to the Narragansett chiefs, and warn them to abstain from hostilities against Uncas and against one another. An expedition, the command of which had been offered to Gen. Denison and declined, had been sent a few years before, under Major Willard, against Ninigret. The result of this had been far from satisfactory. "There having been many messengers to this purpose," say the Massachusetts commissioners, "to the Indian sachems, but seldom observed by them, which now to renew again . . . can in reason have no other attendance in conclusion, than to render us low and contemptible in the eyes of the Indians, or engage us to vindicate our honor in a dangerous and unnecessary war upon Indian quarrels, the grounds whereof we can hardly ever satisfactorily understand."

In 1660, Gen. Denison joined the Ancient and Honorable Artillery Company, and the same year was elected commander, which was the first authentic instance of a person being admitted a member, and the same year admitted to its highest office.

"The monarchy having been now restored in the person of Charles II., the General Court of Massachusetts, apprehending difficulties with the throne, proceeded to take certain precautions. At the close of the session of 1661, Gen. Denison, with others, was appointed a committee to consider and debate such matter or thing of public concernment, touching our patent laws, privileges and duty to his majesty, as they in their wisdom shall deem most expedient, and draw up the result of their apprehensions, and present the same to the next session for consideration and approbation, that so (if the will of God be) we may speak and act the same thing, becoming prudent, honest, conscientious and faithful men."

"The king having made demands of Massachusetts, through Secretary Morrice, among which was one 'express command and charge that four or five influential persons to be chosen by the Governor and Council should be sent to England forthwith, to attend upon his majesty,' the General Court at its session, Sept. 11, 1666, appointed a committee to draw up a letter through Secretary Morrice, giving their reasons for not submitting to the mandates of the royal commissioners sent the year previous, and also replying at length to a proposal for an invasion of New France.

"In the debate, to which this letter gave rise, Gen. Denison and Mr. Bradstreet were much more compliant than the other magistrates, being confirmed in their views, perhaps, by the petitions which had come in from several towns, praying for submission to the king's demands."

"Major-Gen. Denison declared his dissent from the letter to be sent to Secretary Morrice, as not being proportionate to the end desired, and he hopes intended, and desired it might be entered, viz. : Due satisfaction to his majesty and the preservation of the peace and liberty of this colony." "The king's commands pass anywhere," says Denison. "No doubt you may have a trial at law when you come in England if you desire it, and you may insist upon it and claim it. Prerogative is as necessary as law, and is for the good of the whole, that there be always power in being to act, and where there is a right of power, it will be abused so long as 'tis in the hands of weak men, and the less pious the more apt to miscarry ; but right may not be denied because it may be abused. If we shall refuse to answer here to commissioners, and in England also, what will the king say ? Is it not plain that jurisdiction is denied to his majesty ? Though no appeal lies to his majesty so to stop justice but it may require an answer thereto, so that our absolute power to determine must not abate the king's prerogative."

"The capture of New York by the Dutch in 1673, created an alarm among the English colonies, lest their dominion might also be invaded. Accordingly the Federal commissioners met at Hartford and recommended to the General Court of each of the colonies to provide means of defence. The Governor and Council of Massachusetts, at a meeting August 4, 1673, ordered—"that for defence against the Dutch, in case of their appearance before the harbor, endeavors be used to set the three principal forts in order."

"1st. That the honored Governor and Major-General shall be, and hereby is empowered, in case of any notice or appearance or assault of the enemy, to command such company of foot or horse as belong to the regiments of Suffolk, or Middlesex, to come in to the relief of the towns of Boston or Charlestown."

"6. That the Major of Essex regiment, Daniel Denison, Esq., shall and hereby is empowered and required to send relief into Salem and Marblehead."

"In the disastrous war with the Indians which broke upon the colonies in 1675, Gen. Denison, as might be supposed from his position, took an active part. There are several letters extant relating to this latter portion of his life. These for the most part are well preserved, and the handwriting, which is excellent, is as distinct as ever, although two centuries have fled since they were written. He was appointed commander-in-chief of the Massachusetts forces, June, 1675, as may be seen in the instructions given him by the Governor and Council; but as he was prevented by sickness from taking the field, Major Thomas Savage was substituted in his place.

"It would exceed the limits allotted to this sketch to give these official documents in detail. They serve to show that Gen. Denison was skillful with his pen, as well as with his sword, and that the authorities of the colony had the largest confidence in his abilities, and in his fidelity to public trusts."

"Oct. 12, 1676. The court appointed Gen'l Denison to proceed to Portsmouth, and to take chief command of the forces there destined for the war at the eastward.

"He was authorized 'to impress men, horses, ammunition and provisions, and as shall to him seem mete.'"

"In this connection, we extract the following from Hubbard's *Present State of New England:*

"The Governor and Council of the Massachusetts colony had at this time their hands full with the like attempts of Philip and his complices to the westward, yet were not unmindful of the deplorable condition of the eastern Plantations, having committed the care thereof to the respective regiments of the several counties on that side of the country, but more especially to the care and prudence of the honoured Major Daniel Denison, the Major-General of the whole colony, a gentleman who by his great insight in and long experience of all martial affairs was every way accomplished for the managing that whole affair."

"Active operations against the enemy at the eastward were carried on until late in the autumn of 1676, under the direction of Gen. Denison. Magg, the Etcchenmic sachem, surrendered himself to the commander-in-chief at Portsmouth, and was sent to Boston, where a treaty was concluded, stipulating the cessation of hostilities, the restoration of prisoners, etc. This state of peace continued, however, only until the following spring, when hostilities were again commenced, and did not cease until the termination of the war in the spring of 1678. In the year 1677, Denison was not elected to the office of Major-General, but during the remaining years of his life he filled that position. As one of the licensers of the press, with Bradstreet and Dudley, he authorizes the imprint and publication of Hubbard's Narrative, March 29, 1677. In May of this year, he is one of three to grant permission to Indians to carry arms."

"The General Court granted to General Denison, Oct. 10, 1677, an island of 6 or 7 acres, opposite the middle of his farm for his distinguished services."

"Of the remaining years of Gen. Denison's life we know but very little. As he was chosen Assistant the very year his death occurred, we may presume that the distressing disease of which he died did not prevent him from performing the public duties to which he was called until very near the end. It is probable that he occupied the leisure moments of the latter portion of his active life in writing the treatise which he left at his decease, and which was published by his good pastor, Wm. Hubbard, two years after that event. The volume, which is entitled, "*Irenicon, or Salve for New England's Sore*," is exceedingly rare, and is a good specimen of the quaint language of the day.

"In this he considers. 1. What our present maladies are intended in this discourse. 2. What might be the occasion thereof.   3. The danger.   4. The blameable causes.   5. The cure.

" Among the manifold symptoms of this disease, I apprehend none more threatening our dissolution than the sad and unreasonable divisions about matters of religion.   A receipt of these five simples without composition, accompanied with fasting and praying. till they are well digested, with God's blessing. may bring about the expected cure ; for the Dose you need not trouble yourself, there is not danger of taking too much. And if this should fail. which I fear not. I have another receipt, but I fear it is somewhat corroding, which I hope I shall never have occasion to use, my lenitives working according to my expectation.   So I take my leave, committing you to God and a good Nurse."

"During the last month of his life he was called upon to give his opinion in matters relating to the church at Andover."

" Gen. Denison died at Ipswich, Mass., Sept. 20, 1682. The death of so distinguished a public servant must have called forth expressions of grief not alone among his immediate family and townsmen, but throughout the colony.

" It is much to be regretted that we have neither portrait nor description of the person of General Denison ; and of his private worth we glean our knowledge chiefly from the funeral sermon preached by his pastor."

" 'The greater is our sorrow, who are now met together to solemnize the funeral of a person of so great worth, enriched with so many excellencies, which made him live neither undesired nor die unlamented, nor go to his grave unobserved. . . . 'Is there not a prince and a great man fallen this day in Israel?' So, in a sense, it may be said here, a great man is fallen in our little Israel. Concerning the man whose funeral obsequies were lately celebrated amongst us, not to say more than is convenient, to prevent emulation in them that are surviving : His parts and abilities were well known amongst those with whom he lived, and might justly place him among the first three, having indeed many natural advantages above others for the more easy attaining of skill in every science."

" His military skill, some years before his death, advanced him to the conduct and command of the whole, which he was able to have managed with great exactness, yet was he not inferior in other sciences; and as a good soldier of Christ Jesus he had attained to no small confidence in his last conflicts with the king of terrors, being not afraid to look death in the face, in cold blood, but with great composedness of mind received the last summons. For though he was followed with tormenting pain of the stone, or strangury, that pursued him to the last, he neither expressed impatience under those grinding pains nor want of confidence or comfort from his first seizure. . . . So having fought the good fight, run his race and finished his course, he quietly resigned up his spirit to God who gave it. His last thoughts and endeavors were for the good of the public, as may be seen by the *Irenicon*, now lately found among his papers, which, it is thought, would be too much ingratitude to withhold from the view of all any longer."

That his funeral services were conducted in a manner worthy of his distinguished rank and of the high estimation in which he was held, may be judged from the following, copied from the Massachusetts archives:

"WHEREAS, It hath pleased the Lord, in his Sovereign Providence, to take away our honored Daniel Denison, Esq., and in regard to his long continuance a Major-General, it occasioned a very considerable charge at his funeral, and the annual income of his family being but small, the Magistrates judge meet that the Treasurer allow to his widow the full of this year's salary, until May next, and also twenty pounds in money, to be paid the said widow, in pay of her said funeral charges.

"The Magistrates have passed this, their brethren, the Deputy's, hereto consenting.

"EDWARD RAWSON, *Sec'y.*

"*Oct.* 18, 1682.　The Deputys consent not hereto.
"WILLIAM TORREY, *Clerk.*"

"Mrs. Denison survived her husband eight years. Of her life and character we know nothing with certainty. They had two children, John and Elizabeth. John married Martha, daughter of Deputy Governor Symonds, and had three children; one of whom, John, graduated at Harvard College, was chosen as colleague with Mr. Hubbard, at Ipswich, and was much beloved by his people. His life was short. John (senior) died Jan. 9, 1671. Elizabeth married Rev. John Rogers, President of Harvard College.

ADDENDA.

Nancy Burlingame Denison (page 22) died at Vernon Centre, Dec. 24, 1884 and was buried at Floyd, N. Y.

Catherine Denison Baily (page 28) died at Brookfield, N. Y., in 1890.

Milford C. Reed (page 28) died at San Francisco, Cal., Oct. 10, 1893.

Jared J. Bixby (page 29) died March 28, 1881. His widow Mary C. married John C. Loomis in 18—. Resides in Utica, N. Y.

Alexander H. Denison (page 30) died at Copenhagen, N. Y., in 1897.

George Burlingame Denison (page 34) died at Muscatine, Iowa, Dec. 13, 1889.

Edna Denison (page 34) married J. Scott Blackwell Oct. 21, 1891. Has two children, Margaret, born Aug. 5, 1892 ; Bernice, born Oct. 2, 1898. Resides in Muscatine, Iowa.

Cornelia Pond Denison (page 35) died at Whitesboro, N. Y., Feb. 15, 1898. Was buried at Rome, N. Y.

George Ellery Denison (page 35) married Christena Yale Pollock, July 5, 1898. Reside at Whitesboro, N. Y.

Charles Ellery Denison (page 37) married First, Lilly Florence Sweetser, May 12, 1887, she died May 11, 1896, Second, Mary Frances Stivers, Jan. 24, 1899. Reside in New York City.

Ellen Louise Denison (page 37) married Charles
Curtis Pritchard, Feb. 1, 1900. Reside in New
York City.

James M. Colman (page 39) died at Seattle,
Wash., Feb. 8, 1886.

Mary (Colman) Hutchinson (page 39) children :
a daughter, still born Feb. 15, 1884 ; a son, still
born Jan. 1, 1885. Mary Ellen, born Jan. 20, 1886,
died Feb. 3, 1886. Nellie Isabell, born Oct. 9,
1887. William Harrison, born Nov. 18, 1888, died
Dec. 18, 1888. Clara, born Nov. 10, 1889. Eric
Colman, born July 16, 1893, died Sept. 18, 1893.
A daughter, unnamed, born Jan. 22, 1900.

Clara June Colman (page 39) married Richard
H. Simpson May 1, 1891. Children are Hugh
Colman, born Jan. 4, 1892. Gerald Richard, born
Aug. 15, 1893.

Cornelia, born April 1st, 1900, daughter of George E. Denison and Christena Y. Pollock (page 73).

Fred. A. Martin married Alice Groff (page 36).   Children :   Arthur Edwin, born Dec. 12, 1880 ; Gertrude Edna, born Nov. 24, 1882 ; Lottie May, born March 12, 1885 ; Ethel Alice, born and died Aug. 2, 1886 ; Ella Leona, born Sept. 5, 1889 ; James Stanley, born Dec. 19, 1892 , Leslie Lyle, born Jan. 15, 1896.   Reside in Syracuse, N. Y.

Lillie E. Martin (page 36) married James B. Craig, Sept. 29, 1887. Reside in Syracuse, N. Y.

John M. Martin (page 36) married Marie Louise Klugherz, April 17, 1884.   Children :   Emily Lillian, born   April 7, 1885 ; Lulu Helen, born July 14, 1887 ; Edith May, born Dec. 4, 1889 ; John H., born April 7, 1892 : Charles Harvey born Dec. 19, 1893, died May 3, 1894.   Reside in Brooklyn, N. Y.

Millie Maud Martin (page 36) married William Burch, July 31, 1890. Reside at Bear Lake, Penn.

APPENDIX.

RECORD OF THE AMERICAN ANCESTRY OF THE BROTHERS.

George B. Denison, born Feb. 13, 1819; died at Muscatine, Iowa, Dec. 13, 1889.

Charles M. Denison, born April 3, 1822, now living at Whitesboro, N. Y., and

Dr. Ellery Denison, born Dec. 22, 1827, now living at 113 West 12th Street, New York City, sons of Samuel Denison, late of the Town of Floyd, N. Y.

George B. Denison compiled and published in 1881, the Denison Genealogies, 1586-1881. This appendix was compiled by Charles M. Denison, in 1900.

DENISONS.

FIRST GENERATION.

William Denison, born in 1586. Emigrated to America in 1631 and settled at Roxbury, Mass.; died in 1653.

SECOND GENERATION.

Cap't George Denison, born 1618. Was twice married. First to Bridget Thompson, second to Ann Borodell. Came to America with his father, William, settled at Stonington, Conn.; died in 1694.

THIRD GENERATION.

John Denison, born 1646; died in 1698. Settled at Stonington, Conn. Married Phebe Lay, daughter of Robert Lay, of Saybrooke, Conn., Nov. 26, 1667 Robert Lay came from England in 1647 and settled at Saybrooke, Conn.; died in 1695.

FOURTH GENERATION

George Denison, born 1671; died in 1720. Lived in New London, Conn. Married in 1694, Mrs. Mary (Wetherell) Harris, daughter of Daniel Wetherell, of New London, Conn. Mary Wetherell Harris was twice married. She was a great-granddaughter of Elder William Brewster, of the Mayflower. Her mother was Grace Brewster and married Daniel Wetherell, Aug. 4, 1659. Her father was Jonathan Brewster, a son of Elder William Brewster

This record makes George, Charles and Ellery Denison, lineal descendants of Elder William Brewster, as well as of Rev. Wm. Wetherell, the father of Daniel Wetherell.

Miss Caulkins' History of New London, pages 277, 334, 271 and 363, says, "Daniel Wetherell was born Nov. 29, 1630, at the Free School House in Maidstone, Kent, Old England." "Daniel Wetherell, of New London, son of William Wetherell, Clericus of Scituate, was married Aug. 4, 1659, to Grace, daughter of Mr. Jonathan Brewster." (He was a son of William Brewster, called "Elder" Brewster, who came over in the Mayflower.)

" Daniel Wetherell's daughter Mary, born Oct. 7, 1668, married first Thomas Harris, second George Denison, of New London, Conn., in 1694.

In part three of the SIGNERS of the MAYFLOWER Compact, by Annie Arnoux Haxtun, appear numerous records of Elder William Brewster and his descendants. They are known as the Brewster Records. Such as relate to Grace and Hannah, daughters of Jonathan Brewster are given with the page number on which they may be found. Hannah seems to have been twice married.

(Page 13.)

" Daniel Wetherell maryied to Grace Brewster, Aug. 4, 1659.

(Page 14.)

" Note.—The following genealogy comprehends all the important particulars I have found in the " Brewster Records," which was, no doubt, owned by Jonathan Brewster, Elder William Brewster's oldest son. Joseph P. Beach, Cheshire, Conn.

" 1. Elder William Brewster died April 10, 1644. Married Mary————; died, Plymouth, April 17, 1627.

Children :

    2. Johnnathan, born at Scrooby, Aug. 12, 1593; died Aug. 7, 1659. Married Lucretia Oldham, April 10, 1629. (date missing). She died March 4, 1678-79.

Children :

3. William, born March 9, 1625. Married Mary Graeme, Oct. 15, 1651.

4. Mary, born April 16, 1627. Married John Warner, Nov. 10, 1645.

5. Jonathan, born July 17, 1629.

6. Ruth, born Oct. 3, 1631. Married John Pickett, March 14, 1651.

7. Benjamin, born Nov. 17, 1633. Married Anne Parte (should have been Dart,) Feb. 28, 1669.

8. Elizabeth, born May 1, 1637. Married Peter Bradley. Sept. 7, 1653.

9. Grace, born Nov. 1, 1639. Married Daniel Wetherell, Aug. 4, 1659.

10. Hannah, born Nov. 3, 1641."

(Page 15.)

" Daniel Wetherell, ye son of William Wetherell —Clericus of Scituate, in New England—married Grace, the daughter of Jonathan and Grace Brewster, of New London, the 4th of August, 1659."

(Page 15.)

" Samuel Starr was married to Hannah, daughter of Jonathan Brewster, Dec. 25, 1664."

(Page 15.)

" Mary Wetherell, daughter of Daniel and Grace Wetherell, born Oct. 7, 1668."

(Page 32.)

" Miss Caulkin, in her History of New London, states that Hannah (Daughter of Jonathan) married, Dec. 25, 1664, Samuel Starr. She was aged 37 in 1680.

Kind fate, which in its workings seems like Providence, brought Miss Elizabeth Miner Avery, of Groton, Conn., to my department, and as a part of the toll, the whole world of my knowledge has been obliged to pay I immediately proposed to her the questions in regard to Hannah Brewster, so near to my heart.

She wrote me the last of 1897, giving me the following : "I copy from the Starr Genealogy, prepared by Burgess Starr Pratt, Hartford, 1879. The first mention of Samuel Starr in New London is his marriage, Dec. 25, 1664, with Hannah, daughter of Jonathan Brewster. She was born 1643. Nov. 25, 1691, was in full communion with the first Church in New London, where her children were baptised. No record of her death. The children of Samuel and Hannah Starr were, Samuel, born Dec. 11, 1665. Thomas, born Sept. 27, 1668. Comfort, born Aug. 7, 1671. Jonathan, born Feb. 23, 1673-4.

This is the same as Miss Caulkin's History.

(Page 32.)

"While he had no authority there was one item with a bearing on the case at least strong enough to have found place in his note-book. Soon the name of one furnishing it was forthcoming, and from Mrs. A. G. B. Hatch, I have with the names of Jonathan Brewster's children, Hannah, born 1643, married John Thompson, of Shetucket, Thames, Conn., Dec. 25, 1664, married Samuel Starr.

(Page 33.)

"The Rev. Nathaniel Brewster returned to Setauket in 1665, having spent two or three years in other places, as I have already written. At the close of 1664, Hannah Brewster married Samuel Starr, and was ready and willing to give up the charge of her nephews to their legitimate guardians. Her life in regard to John Thompson was a thing of the past, and new duties awaited her and from that time her movements were recorded. Thus I have told all I know. In gaining this information I have become an historical beggar, seeking of everyone the smallest morsel of knowledge in their possession."

Elder William Brewster was one of the most distinguished of the many prominent emigrants from the old to the new world. This is his biography, as it appears on page 122 of Drake's Dictionary of American Biography.

"BREWSTER, William, a Pilgrim of Plymouth, elder and only teacher for some years, b. Scrooby, Eng., in 1566. d. Plymouth, Ms. April 16, 1644. After an education at Cambridge U., he entered the service of William Davison, ambassador of Queen Elizabeth, in Holland, between whom and himself a strong attachment subsisted.

"Through Davison's influence, he was made Postmaster of Scrooby. Turning his attention to religious subjects, he withdrew from the established church, and established with others a separate society. This new church met on the Lord's day, at Mr. Brewster's house, as long as they could assemble without interruption. Endeavoring by flight to avoid their persecutors, Mr. Brewster and Mr. Bradford and others, were seized in 1607, just as they were going to Holland and imprisoned at Boston in Lincolnshire. Mr. Brewster, having most property, was the greatest sufferer, and obtaining with much difficulty and expense his liberty, he first assisted the poor of the society to emigrate and then followed them to Holland. His means being exhausted, he opened a school at Leyden for teaching the English language. By the assistance of some friends, he also procured a printing press, and published several books against the hierarchy, but could not obtain a license for their publication in England. Such was his reputation in the church at Leyden that he was chosen a ruling elder, and accompanied its members who emigrated to New England in 1620. The church at Plymouth being for several years destitute of a minister, Mr. Brewster, who was respected for his character and venerable age, frequently officiated as a preacher, though he could never be persuaded to administer the sacraments."

See Life and Times of William Brewster, by A. Steel, 1857.

See Vol. 3, American Cyclopedia, page 263.

See also Part I, Signers of the Mayflower Compact by Mrs. Haxtun, pages 11, 12, 13, 14.

FIFTH GENERATION.

Daniel Denison, born 1703; died previous to 1780. Lived in New London, Conn. Married Rachel

Starr, Nov. 14, 1726. She was a daughter of Thomas Starr, son of Samuel Starr and Hannah Brewster, married Dec. 23, 1664. Hannah was the daughter of Jonathan Brewster, who was the son of Elder William Brewster. See page 277 Calkins' History of New London. See page 34, Sweet's Averys.

This is the second trace back to Elder William Brewster of the Mayflower, as well as a trace to the Starr family.

Sixth Generation.

Daniel Denison, Jr.; born in 1730. Moved from New London, Conn., to Stephentown, N. Y.; died in 1793. Married Katherine Avery, July 1, 1756. Katherine was the daughter of Col. Ebenezer Avery, born in 1704, who was the son of James Avery 3rd, born in 1673, who was a son of James Avery, Jr., born in 1646, who was a son of Cap't James Avery, born in 1620, the head of the Groton Averys.

See Sweet's Genealogy of Groton Averys.

Daniel Denison, Jr., was a soldier in the Revolution.

Seventh Generation.

Samuel Denison, born in 1774. Settled in Floyd, N. Y., in 1800; died there Dec. 11, 1849. Was twice married, the second time in 1817 to Nancy Burlingame, daughter of Freeborn and Lydia (Bacon) Burlingame, of Providence, R. I.

Eighth Generation.

George B., Charles M., and Ellery Denison.

CHILTONS LATHAMS & WINSLOWS.

More recent investigations make it manifest that Lucy Latham was not a descendant of James Chilton. Under date of April 27th, 1900, Miss Elizabeth Miner Avery, of Groton, Conn., writes me :

" Permit me to enclose to you my record of the Latham family, collected from family, town and other reliable records. I would be glad to descend from Mary Chilton and the Winslows, but at the same time should be most sorry to give up Carie Latham and his sonorous boatsman's voice, who " has the honor of being the first permanent white settler in Groton," and whose " ferry lot " is still owned by his descendants."

RECORD.

(1) " Carie, or Cary, or Kary Latham, born in England 1612, died 1695. Married in 1638 Elizabeth, daughter of John and Jane Masters, of Watertown, and relic of Edward Lockwood. Cary Latham probably married in Boston as the births of two of his children are recorded there. There were seven children."

(2) " Joseph, second child of Cary and Elizabeth Masters-Lockwood-Latham, was born Dec. 2d, 1642 as recorded in Boston, died at New London, (or Groton) 1706. Married Mary- This marriage is not recorded in New London, probably took place in Newfoundland. They had 11 children. Cary the first child was born at Newfoundland July 14th, 1668."

(3) " William Latham, second child of Joseph and Mary Latham, born July 9th, 1670, died Nov. 5th, 1732. Married June 30th, 1698 Hannah Morgan, of Groton. They had six children."

(4) " Lucy Latham, fifth child of William and Hannah Morgan Latham, born May 21st, 1709, died May 2d, 1758. Married Colonel Ebenezer Avery, June 16, 1726, and was mother of all his twelve children.

Rachel Starr Denison, Col. Avery's second wife, was cousin to Lucy Latham through the Morgans."

CHARLES M. DENISON,

WHITESBORO, N. Y.

GRISWOLDS.

James Avery 3rd. married Mary Griswold in 1696. She was a daughter of Matthew Griswold, founder of the town of Lyme.

CHILTONS, LATHAMS AND WINSLOWS.

Col. Ebenezer Avery, son of James Avery 3rd, and Mary Griswold, married 1726, Lucy Latham, daughter of Joseph Latham. Latham is a common name among the Averys. I have not the records with which to correctly trace the Lathams back to the emigrant.

Lucy Latham, as I have it by tradition, was a lineal descendant of James Chilton. He was one of the Signers of the Mayflower Compact and came over in that ship, accompanied by his wife and daughter, Mary. Mary married John Winslow, brother of Gov. Edward Winslow. Their daughter, Susanna Winslow, married Robert Latham, of Bridgewater, in 1649. Joseph Latham, Lucy Latham's father, it is said, was a descendant of Susanna Winslow and Robert Latham. If this is so, then the descendants of Daniel Denison, Jr. (6), and Katherine Avery, daughter of Col. Ebenezer Avery, have a third trace back to the Mayflower pilgrims.

> See Mrs. Haxtun's Signers of the Mayflower Compact, Part II, page 24.

Mrs. Haxtun gives the name as Roger Latham. This is a mistake, doubtless, of the compositor. The following excerpts from records have been kindly furnished me by Miss Anne D. Proctor, of Utica, N. Y.

"Robert Latham is in all the books of reference."

> See Davis Landmarks of Plymouth.
> Austin's Rhode Island Families.
> Mitchell's Bridgewater.
> Savage's Gen. Dictionary.

From Mitchell's History of Bridgewater.

"Robert Latham was a constable at Marshfield, 1643. Was at Cambridge two years in Rev. Thomas Shepard's family. Was son, probably, of William, and Cary Latham might have been his uncle. He married Susanna, daughter of John Winslow, brother of Gov. Edward Winslow, 1649, and had the following children:

> Mercy, born 1650, (at Plymouth) married Isaac Harris, (of Rhode Island) probably.
> Joseph, was at Providence, 1690 and 1703, (wife Phebe, signed a Deed 1688.)
> Elizabeth, married Francis Cook.
> Hannah, married Joseph Washburn.
> Sarah, married John Howard, Jr.

"Robert Latham took the oath of fidelity at Marshfield, 1657. Settled at East Bridgewater before 1667. His wife's mother was the famous Mary Chilton, who is said to have been the first female (some say the first person) who set foot on the Plymouth shore, 1620. Her father, James Chilton, and her mother, Susanna, both died the first Winter."

"Joseph Latham, son of Robert and Susanna (Winslow) Latham, was at Providence, R. I., 1690, and 1703. His wife Phebe, signed a Deed 1688."

Page 231, Mitchell's History of Bridgewater.

Page 259, Miss Caulkin's History of New London.

"Patents granted of New London to many people of whom Joseph Latham was one, Oct. 14, 1704.

"Phebe, daughter of Arthur and Mary (Waterman) Fenner, married Joseph Latham, son of Robert and Susanna (Winslow) Latham.

Children, born in Rhode Island: Robert, Sarah, Phebe.

Page 74, Austin's Rhode Island Families.

Fenner lineage is fine. Providence, R. I.

In these places only the children, born there have registration. Lucy in some other place, probably, as a Susanna is mentioned.

Page 261, Austin's Rhode Island Families.

"1693, October 10th, James and John Brown, of Newport, sold Joseph Latham, of Providence, 30 acres of land for nine pounds.

Page 315.

"Toleration Harris remembers Susanna Latham very handsomely in his will, proved Feb. 9, 1767. This Susanna, probably the daughter of Joseph Latham, and from dates may have been sister of Lucy Latham."

Mary Chilton married John Winslow. Susanna
Winslow married Robert Latham.   Joseph Latham
married Phebe Fenner. So far is confirmed by
Davis's Plymouth, Mitchell's Bridgewater and Austin's Rhode Island Families as already given.

Probably, Col. Ebenezer Avery married 1726,
Lucy Latham, daughter of Joseph Latham.   I find
in Wyman's Charlestown, Mass., there were Lathams in Groton, Conn., as late as 1808, and Lucy
might have been recorded there in 1726.

From Ancient Landmarks of Plymouth, by William T. Davis,
   page 168.

"William Latham came in the Mayflower, and
about 1640, went to England and then to Bahamas,
where he is said to have died."
Page 51.

"James Chilton came in the Mayflower with wife
and child Mary, who married John Winslow.   He
died in Princetown, and his wife in Plymouth soon
after landing.   Another daughter married in England, and, following her parents, was living in Plymouth in 1650."
Page 290, Winslow:

John, son of 1st Edward (who came in the Mayflower) came in the Fortune, 1621, and married
about 1627, Mary, daughter of James Chilton, who
came in the Mayflower, 1620, and had Susanna,
who married Robert Latham.   They had a daughter Hannah Latham, who married Joseph Wash-
burn, of Bridgewater, Mass., son of John (2) Wash-
burn (son of 1st John) who married Elizabeth,
daughter of Experience Mitchell, 1645.

Mary Chilton married John Winslow.

Susanna Winslow married Robert Latham.

SUMMARY OF LINES OF DESCENT.

DENISON.

1st.   William Denison (1), George (2), John (3), George (4), Daniel (5), Daniel Jr., (6), Samuel (7), George B., Charles M., and Ellery (8).

BREWSTER.

2nd.   Elder William Brewster (1), Jonathan (2), Grace Wetherell *nee* Brewster (3), Mary Denison *nee* Wetherell (4), Daniel Denison (5), Daniel Jr., (6), Samuel (7), George B., Charles M., and Ellery (8).

Also, Elder William Brewster (1), Jonathan Brewster (2), Hannah Starr *nee* Brewster (3), Thomas Starr (4), Rachel Denison *nee* Starr (5), Daniel Denison, Jr., (6), Samuel (7), George B., Charles M., and Ellery (8).

The Denison cousins, who are lineal descendants of Elder William Brewster, are very numerous.

There are recorded on pages 34 to 60 inclusive, of Baldwin & Cliff's Genealogy of Cap't George Denison, of Stonington, Conn., published in 1881, the names of some Six Hundred and Fifty.

AVERY.

3rd. James Avery (1), James, Jr., (2) James 3rd
(3), Col. Ebenezer (4), Katherine Denison *nee*
Avery (5), Samuel Denison (6), George B.,
Charles M., and Ellery (7).

LAY.

4th. Robert Lay (1), Phebe Denison *nee* Lay (2),
George Denison (3), Daniel Denison (4), Dan-
iel Denison, Jr., (5), Samuel (6), George B.,
Charles M., and Ellery (7).

STARR.

5th. Samuel Starr (1), Thomas Starr (2), Rachel
Denison *nee* Starr (3), Daniel Denison, Jr.,
(4), Samuel Denison (5), George B., Charles
M., and Ellery (6).

WETHERELL.

6th. Rev. Wm. Wetherell (1), Daniel Wetherell
(2), Mary Harris Denison *nee* Wetherell (3),
Daniel Denison (4), Daniel Denison, Jr., (5),
Samuel (6), George B., Charles M., and Ellery
(7).

GRISWOLD.

7th. Griswold, the emigrant (1), Matthew Gris-
wold (2), Mary Avery *nee* Griswold, wife of
James Avery 3rd (3), Col. Ebenezer Avery
(4), Katherine Denison *nee* Avery (5), Samuel
Denison (6), George B., Charles M., and
Ellery (7).

.

www.ingramcontent.com/pod-product-compliance
Lightning Source LLC
Chambersburg PA
CBHW032357280326
41935CB00008B/601